James V. Coombs

Gospel Call

choice songs for revivals, Sunday-schools and the church

James V. Coombs

Gospel Call

choice songs for revivals, Sunday-schools and the church

ISBN/EAN: 9783337265632

Printed in Europe, USA, Canada, Australia, Japan

Cover: Foto ©Lupo / pixelio.de

More available books at **www.hansebooks.com**

THE

GOSPEL CALL;

Choice Songs for

Revivals, Sunday-Schools and the Church.

—BY—

J. V. COOMBS AND W. E. M. HACKLEMAN.

PRICE, Single Copy, by *Mail*, 25 cts.; per Hundred, $20.

PUBLISHED BY
CHRISTIAN PUBLISHING COMPANY, ST. LOUIS.
GOSPEL CALL PUB. CO., INDIANAPOLIS, IND.

Copyrighted by J. V. Coombs, Irvington, Ind.

PREFACE.

In offering "THE GOSPEL CALL" for public favor, we desire to call attention to a few important features:

1. We have used no worthless pieces merely to fill up the book. All songs are to be used. We asked a music firm for permission to use one selection. The reply was: "You can use it for $25. The book from which it is taken sells on account of three or four good songs. One good hymn carries fifty worthless ones." This firm confesses that forty-nine out of fifty of their songs are worthless. Why buy 800 or 900 songs in order to get twenty or thirty?

2. We have selected but 185 hymns, 100 entirely new songs; 50 choice songs, suitable for Gospel meetings, revivals and Sunday schools, and 35 standard hymns, dear to every Christian. The evangelist can find the book he needs in the Gospel Call.

3. Each year every Sunday-school wants a new book, no matter how good the book in use. Many schools cannot afford to purchase the costly books. We furnish the GOSPEL CALL from 33 to 50 per cent cheaper than ordinary Sunday-school and church books.

4. We have secured a few songs from the leading musicians in the land.

5. Books for Sunday-schools are generally filled with light, frivolous music. We have selected both words and music with reference to the wants of the church. The GOSPEL CALL may, therefore, be used in Sunday-schools, church or gospel meetings.

6. Books of this nature generally sell for from 35 cents to 60 cents per copy. We furnish the GOSPEL CALL for 25 cents a copy.

Trusting that this little book may cause many to "sing with the spirit, and with the understanding" also, we send the GOSPEL CALL on its mission of love.

THE AUTHORS.

THE GOSPEL CALL.

1. That's Enough For Me.

M. W. S.   M. W. SPENCER.

1. I know not what's before me, My way I can-not see,
2. Though friends may all forsake me, And earth-ly com-forts flee,
3. I may be poor and need-y, My home may hum-ble be,
4. Tho' fall the tears of sor-row, Let grief my por-tion be,

But I know that Je-sus leads me, And that's e-nough for me.
There's one who'll never leave me, And that's e-nough for me.
I've a pal-ace o-ver yon-der, That's wealth e-nough for me.
I've Je-sus ev-er with me, That's joy e-nough for me.

CHORUS.

And that's e-nough for me, And that's e-nough for me,
Yes that's e-nough, yes that's e-nough,

But I know that Jesus leads me, And that's e-nough for me.
There's one who'll never leave me, And that's e-nough for me.
I've a pal-ace o-ver yon-der, That's wealth e-nough for me.
I've Je-sus ev-er with me, That's joy e-nough for me.

By per. of "The Echo Music Co."

3. At the Cross.

The blood of Jesus Christ His Son cleanseth from all sin—1 John 1: 7.

R. E. HUDSON.

1. A-las! and did my Sav-ior bleed And did my Sovereign die,
2. Was it for crimes that I have done, He groan'd upon the tree?
3. But drops of grief can ne'er re-pay The debt of love I owe;

Would He de-vote that sa-cred head For such a worm as I?
A-maz-ing pit-y, grace unknown, And love be-yond de-gree!
Here, Lord, I give my-self a-way, 'Tis all that I can do!

CHORUS.

At the cross, at the cross, where I first saw the light, And the bur-den of my heart roll'd a-way— roll'd a-way, It was there by faith I re-ceived my sight, And now I am hap-py all the day.

Copyright, 1885, by R. E. Hudson.

4. The Best Friend is Jesus.

P. B.　　　　　　　　　　　　　　　　　　　　　　　　P. BILHORN.

The Best Friend is Jesus. Concluded.

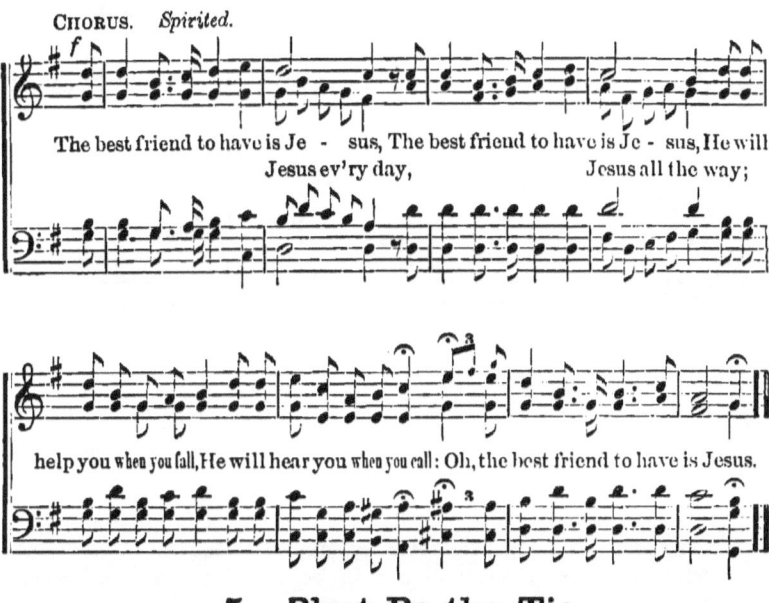

5. Blest Be the Tie.

H. G. NAGELI.

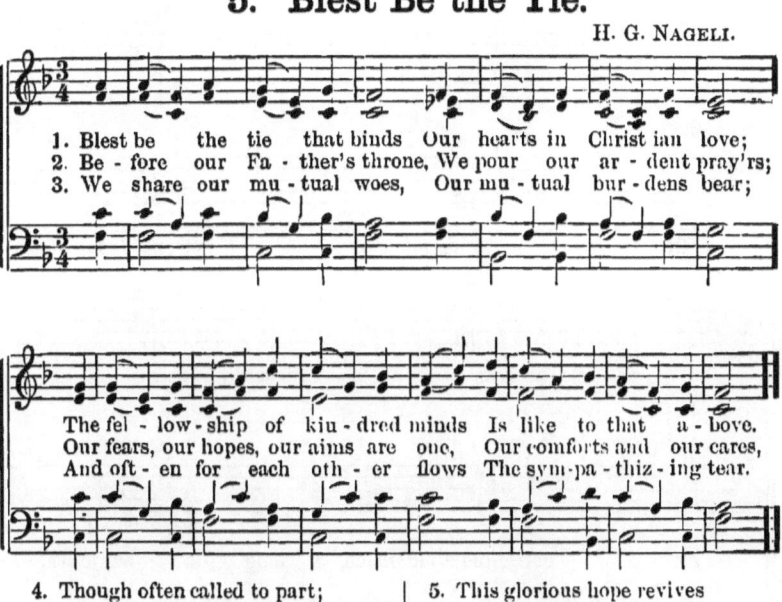

1. Blest be the tie that binds Our hearts in Christian love;
   The fellowship of kindred minds Is like to that above.
2. Before our Father's throne, We pour our ardent pray'rs;
   Our fears, our hopes, our aims are one, Our comforts and our cares,
3. We share our mutual woes, Our mutual burdens bear;
   And often for each other flows The sympathizing tear.

4. Though often called to part;
   Amid these scenes of pain;
   Yet we shall still be joined in heart,
   And hope to meet again.

5. This glorious hope revives
   Our courage by the way;
   Which each in expectation lives,
   And longs to see the day.

7. Healing at the Fountain.

FANNY J. CROSBY.   WM. J. KIRKPATRICK, by per.

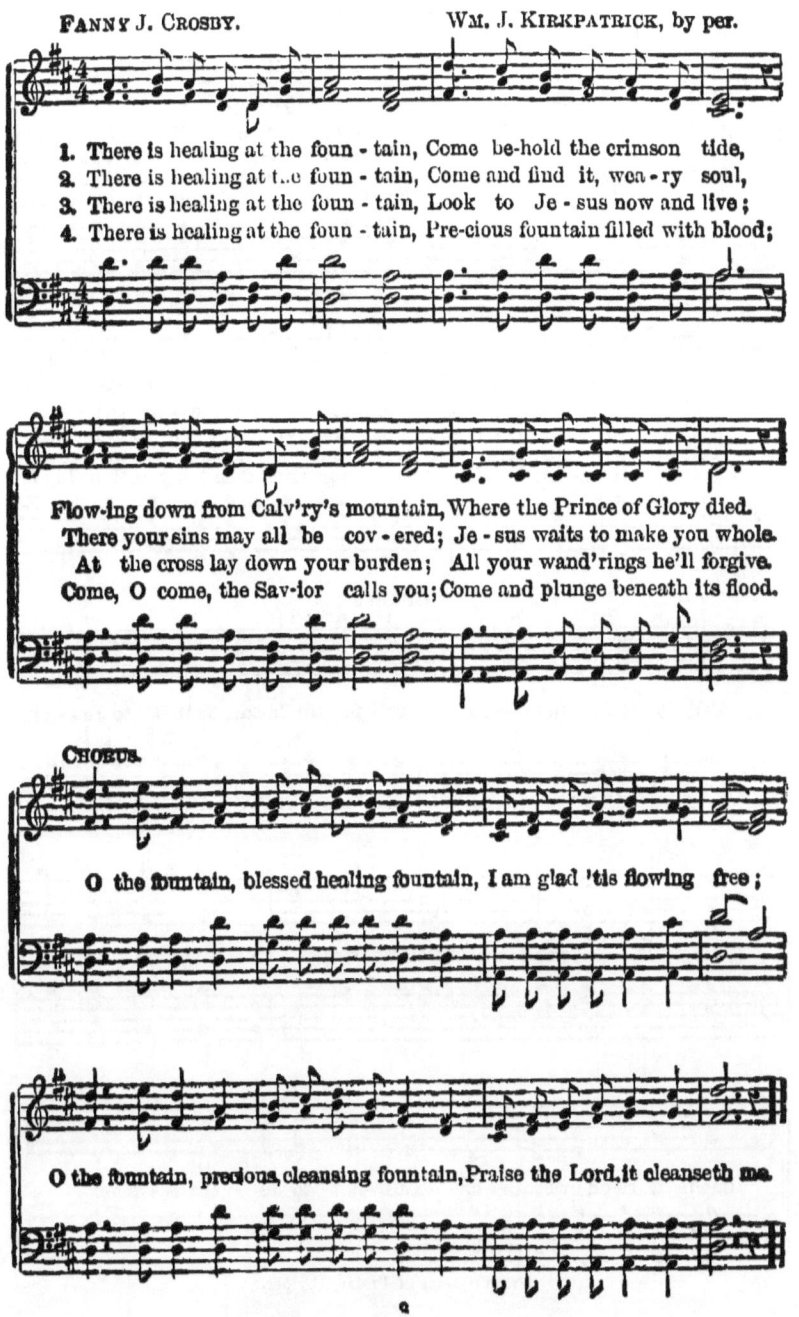

1. There is healing at the foun - tain, Come be-hold the crimson tide,
2. There is healing at the foun - tain, Come and find it, wea - ry soul,
3. There is healing at the foun - tain, Look to Je - sus now and live;
4. There is healing at the foun - tain, Pre-cious fountain filled with blood;

Flow-ing down from Calv'ry's mountain, Where the Prince of Glory died.
There your sins may all be cov - ered; Je - sus waits to make you whole.
At the cross lay down your burden; All your wand'rings he'll forgive.
Come, O come, the Sav-ior calls you; Come and plunge beneath its flood.

CHORUS.

O the fountain, blessed healing fountain, I am glad 'tis flowing free;

O the fountain, precious, cleansing fountain, Praise the Lord, it cleanseth me.

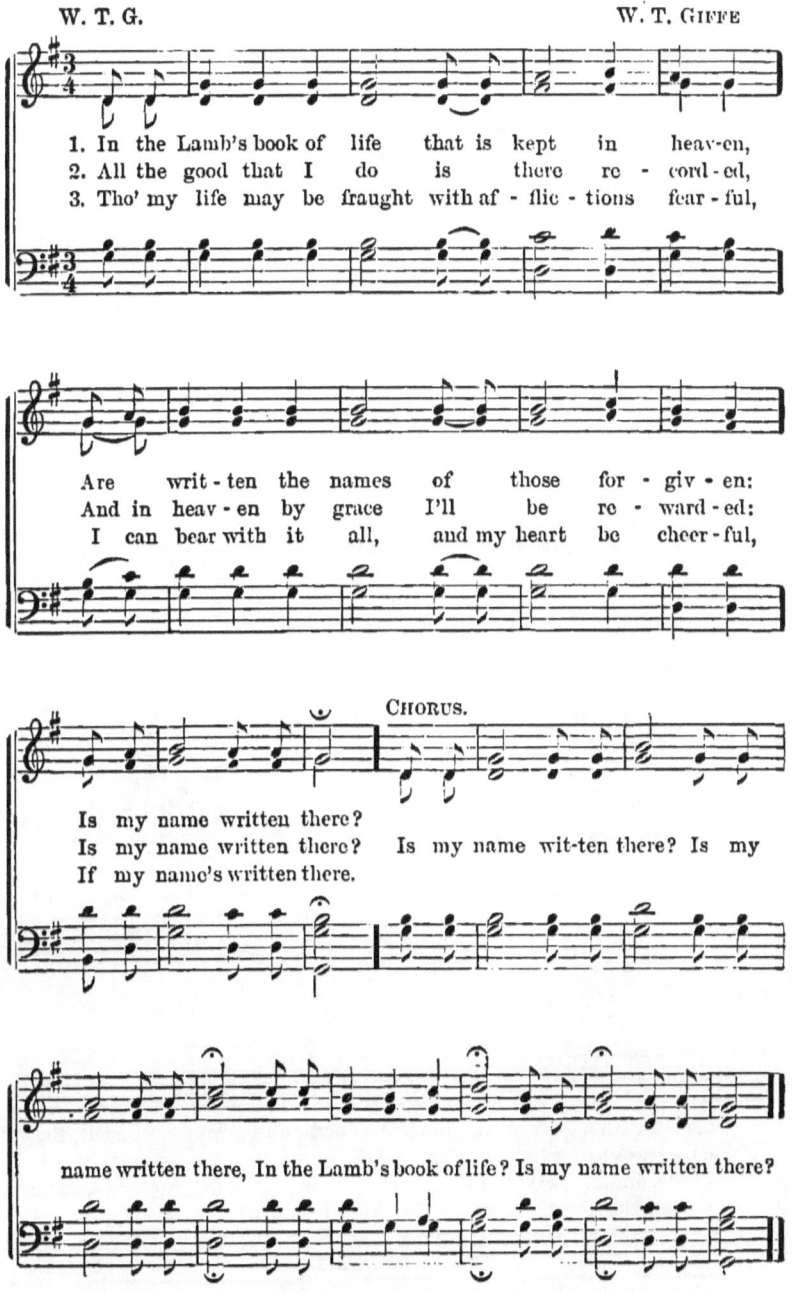

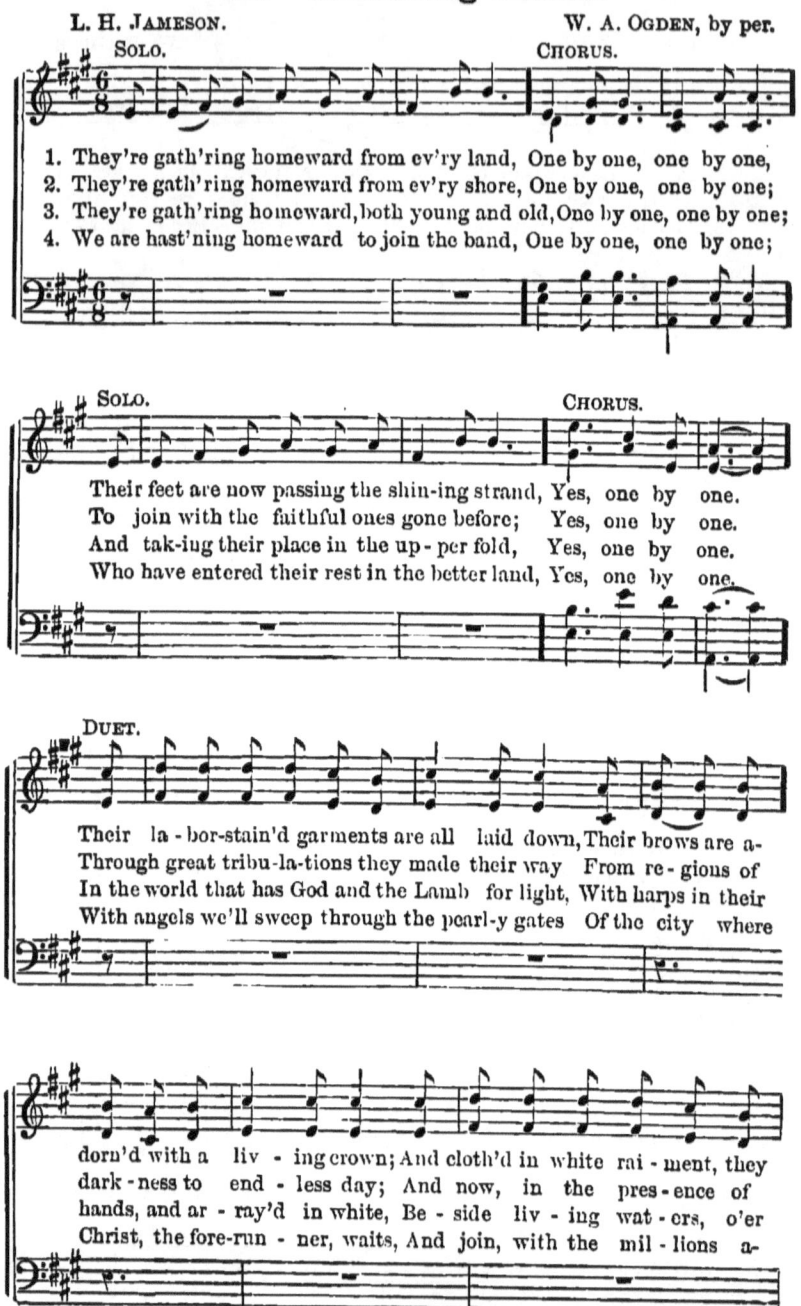

Gathering Home—Concluded.

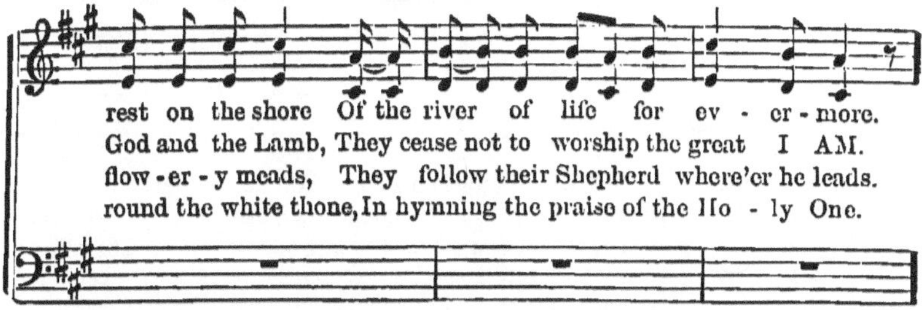

rest on the shore Of the river of life for ev - er - more.
God and the Lamb, They cease not to worship the great I AM.
flow - er - y meads, They follow their Shepherd where'er he leads.
round the white thone, In hymning the praise of the Ho - ly One.

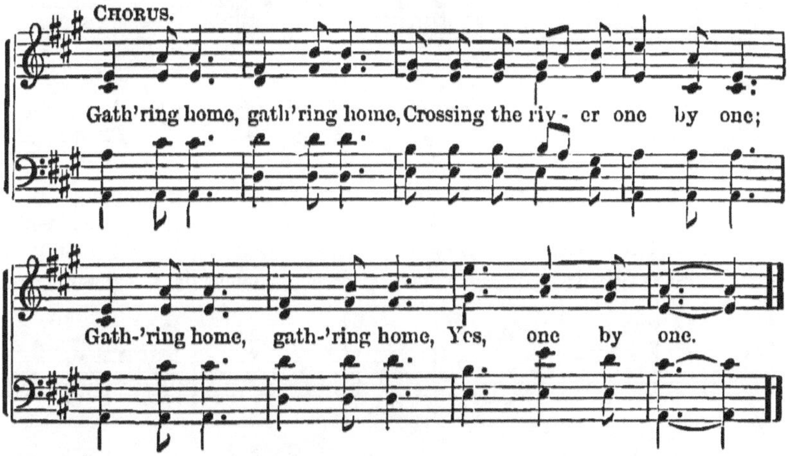

CHORUS.

Gath'ring home, gath'ring home, Crossing the riv - er one by one;

Gath-'ring home, gath-'ring home, Yes, one by one.

11. Come to Jesus.

1. Come to Je - sus, Come to Je - sus, Come to Je - sus just now,
Just now come to Je - sus, Come to Je - sus just now.

2. He will save you.
3. Oh, believe him.
4. He is able.
5. He is willing.
6. He'll receive you.
7. Call upon him.
8. He will hear you.
9. Look unto him.
10. He'll forgive you.
11. Flee to Jesus.
12. Only trust him.
13. Jesus loves you.
14. Don't reject him.
15. I believe him.
16. Hallelujah, Amen.

Then Rejoice, All Ye Ransomed. Concluded.

dead's alive, the lost is found, and wand'rers Now are com-ing, com-ing home.

13. Olivet.

RAY PALMER.   Dr. L. MASON.

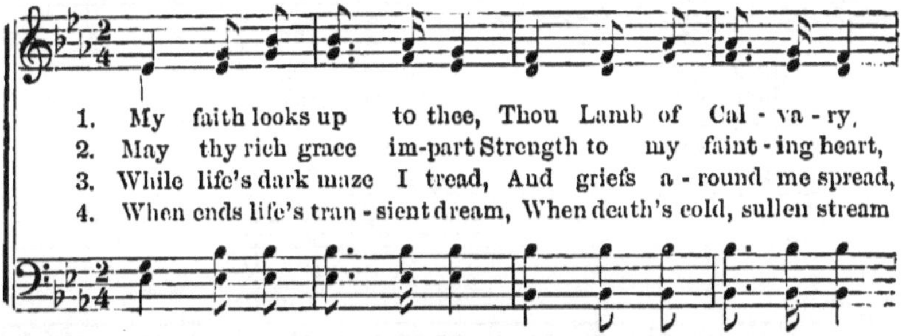

1. My faith looks up to thee, Thou Lamb of Cal-va-ry,
2. May thy rich grace im-part Strength to my faint-ing heart,
3. While life's dark maze I tread, And griefs a-round me spread,
4. When ends life's tran-sient dream, When death's cold, sullen stream

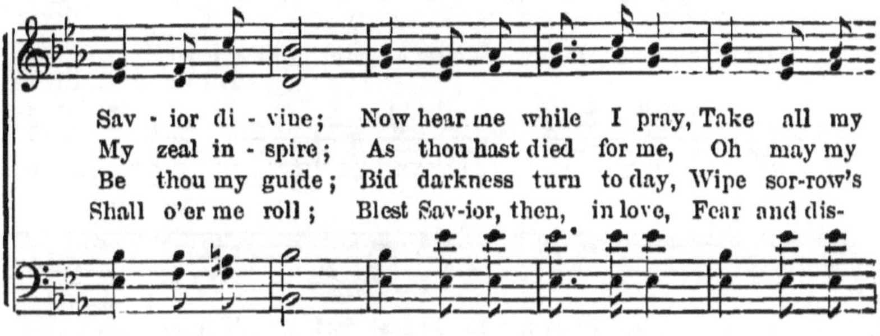

Sav-ior di-vine; Now hear me while I pray, Take all my
My zeal in-spire; As thou hast died for me, Oh may my
Be thou my guide; Bid darkness turn to day, Wipe sor-row's
Shall o'er me roll; Blest Sav-ior, then, in love, Fear and dis-

guilt a-way, Oh, let me from this day Be whol-ly thine.
love to thee Pure, warm, and changeless be,—A liv-ing fire.
tears a-way, Nor let me ev-er stray From thee a-side.
tress remove; O bear me safe above,—A ransomed soul.

16. There's a Great Day Coming.

W. L. T.   W. L. Thompson.

1. There's a great day coming, A great day coming, There's a great day coming by and by, When the saints and the sinners shall be part-ed right and left, Are you read-y for that day to come?
2. There's a bright day coming, A bright day coming, There's a bright day coming by and by, But its bright-ness shall on-ly come to those who love the Lord, Are you read-y for that day to come?
3. There's a sad day coming, A sad day coming, There's a sad day coming by and by, When the sin-ner shall hear his doom, "De-part! I know ye not," Are you read-y for that day to come?

CHORUS.

Are you read-y? Are you read-y? Are you read-y for the Judg-ment day?

By permission of WILL. L. THOMPSON, East Liverpool, Ohio.

There's a Great Day Coming—Concluded.

Are you read-y? Are you read-y For the Judgment day?

17. Revive Us Again.

Dr. W. P. MACKAY. English Melody.

1. We praise thee, O God! for the Son of thy love,
2. We praise thee, O God! for thy Spir-it of light,
3. All glo-ry and praise to the Lamb that was slain,
4. All glo-ry and praise to the God of all grace,
5. Re-vive us a-gain; fill each heart with thy love;

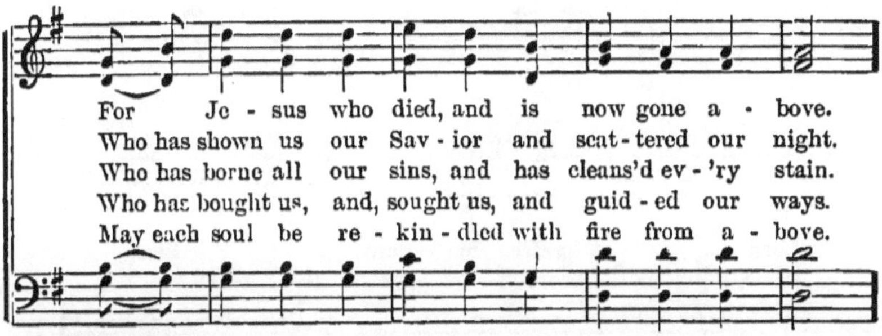

For Je-sus who died, and is now gone a-bove.
Who has shown us our Sav-ior and scat-tered our night.
Who has borne all our sins, and has cleans'd ev-'ry stain.
Who has bought us, and, sought us, and guid-ed our ways.
May each soul be re-kin-dled with fire from a-bove.

CHORUS.

Hallelujah! Thine the glory, Hallelujah! A-men. Revive us a-gain.

The Home For Me—Concluded.

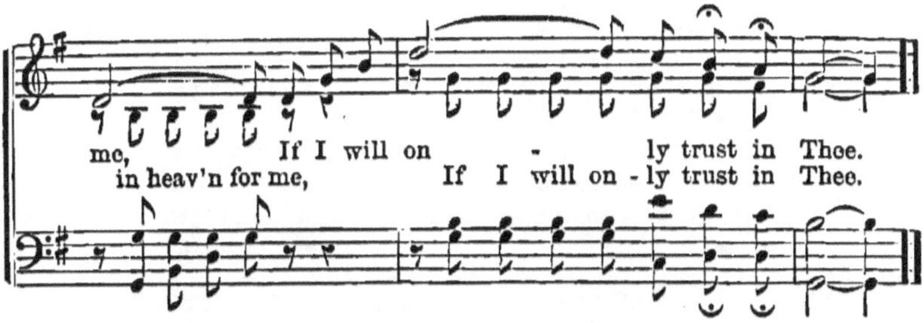

me, If I will on - ly trust in Thee.
in heav'n for me, If I will on - ly trust in Thee.

23. Happy Day.

PHILIP DODDRIDGE.

1. O hap-py day that fixed my choice On thee, my Sav-ior and my God!
Well may this glowing heart re-joice, And tell its raptures all a-broad.
2. O hap-py bond, that seals my vows, To him who mer-its all my love!
Let cheerful an-thems fill his house, While to that sacred shrine I move.

Fine

Hap-py day, hap-py day, When Je-sus washed my sins a-way;
D. S. Hap-py day hap-py day, When Je-sus washed my sins a-way

D.S.

He taught me how to watch and pray, And live re-joic-ing ev-'ry day.

3. 'Tis done, the great transaction's done,
I am my Lord's, and he is mine;
He drew me, and I followed on,
Charmed to confess the voice divine.

4. Now rest, my long divided heart,
Fixed on this blissful centre, rest;
Nor ever from thy Lord depart,
With him of every good possessed.

25. Oh, When Shall I See Jesus?

JOHN LELAND.   G. J. WEBB.

1. Oh, when shall I see Jesus, And dwell with him a-bove,
2. But now I am a sol-dier, My Cap-tain's gone be-fore;
3. Thro' grace I am de-ter-mined To con-quer, tho' I die;

To drink the flow-ing foun-tain Of ev-er-last-ing love?
He's giv-en me my or-ders, And tells me not to fear,
And then a-way to Je-sus On wings of love I'll fly.

When shall I be de-liv-ered From this vain world of sin,
And if I hold out faith-ful, A crown of life he'll give,
Fare-well to sin and sor-row—I bid them both a-dieu;

And with my bless-ed Je-sus Drink end-less pleasures in?
And all his val-iant sol-diers E-ter-nal life shall have.
And you, my friends, prove faith-ful, And on your way pur-sue

4. And if you meet with troubles
And trials on the way,
Then cast your care on Jesus,
And don't forget to pray.
Gird on the heavenly armor
Of faith, and hope, and love,
And when your warfare's ended,
You'll reign with him above.

5. Oh, do not be discouraged,
For Jesus is your friend;
And if you long for knowledge,
On him you may depend.
Neither will he upbraid you,
Though often you request;
He'll give you grace to conquer,
And take you home to rest.

Workers At Home—Concluded.

Who will an-swer, glad-ly say-ing, "Here am I, O Lord: send me?"
You can tell the love of Je-sus, You can say he died for all.
An-swer quick-ly when he call-eth, "Here am I, O Lord: send me."

27. Rock of Ages.

A. M. TOPLADY. THOS. HASTINGS.

1. Rock of a-ges! cleft for me, Let me hide my-self in Thee;
2. Could my tears for-ev-er flow, Could my zeal no lan-guor know'
3. While I draw this fleet-ing breath, When my eyes shall close in death,

Let the wa-ter and the blood, From thy wounded side which flow'd,
These for sin could not a-tone; Thou must save, and thou a-lone:
When I rise to worlds unknown, And be-hold Thee on Thy throne,

Be of sin the doub-le cure, Save from wrath and make me pure.
In my hand no price I bring, Sim-ply to thy cross I cling.
Rock of a-ges! cleft for me, Let me hide my-self in Thee.

28. Crown Him Lord of All.

Spirited.   J. T. REESE.

1. All hail the pow'r of Je-sus name, Let an-gels pros-trate fall;
2. Let ev-'ry kin-dred ev-'ry tribe, On this ter-res-trial ball;
3. Oh, that with yon-der sa-cred throng, We at his feet may fall;

Bring forth the roy-al di-a-dem, And crown him Lord of all.
To him all maj-es-ty as-cribe, And crown him Lord of all.
we'll join the ev-er-last-ing song, And crown him Lord of all.

CHORUS.

We'll crown... him, we'll crown.. him, We'll crown him Lord of all,
We'll crown him   we'll crown him,

We'll crown.. him, we'll crown.. him, We'll crown him Lord of all.
We'll crown him,   we'll crown him,

31. Jesus is Calling To-Day.

D. R. Lucas. J. H. Rosecrans, by per.

Copyright, 1886, by Fillmore Bros.

32. Sailing o'er the Sea.

J. T. REESE

1. We're a faithful pilgrim band, Sailing to the heav'nly land, With a swelling sail we onward sweep; Tho' the tempest rages long, There is one amid the throng, Who will guide the sailor o'er the deep.
2. Tho' the rolling billows swell, Yet, securely we may dwell, Tho' the breakers roar upon the lea; 'Mid the storm by day, or night, If we trust our Captain's might, He will guide us safely o'er the sea.
3. Tho' for many ages past, She has long withstood the blast, And in safety crossed the billows o'er, Yet amid the rocks and shoals, She has landed many souls, On fair Canaan's bright and peaceful shore.

CHORUS.

We are sailing o'er the sea, We are sailing o'er the sea;
Sailing o'er the sea, sailing o'er the sea;

drifting with the tide; Soon the
Drifting with the tide; drifting with the tide;

SAILING O'ER THE SEA.—Concluded.

storms will all be o-ver, And we'll safe-ly reach the oth-er side.

33. HAPPY CHILDREN.

J. V. C. J. V. COOMBS.

1. We are a band of happy, happy children, Singing all day long,
2. Come, let us sing with merry, merry voi-ces, About the Saviour's love,
3. May we all sing around the throne in glo-ry, With the an-gel throng,

Praising the name of the bless-ed Re-deemer, With our hap-py song.
He is preparing a place for his children In his home a-bove.
And join our voices in tell-ing the sto-ry, Singing the new, new song.

CHORUS.

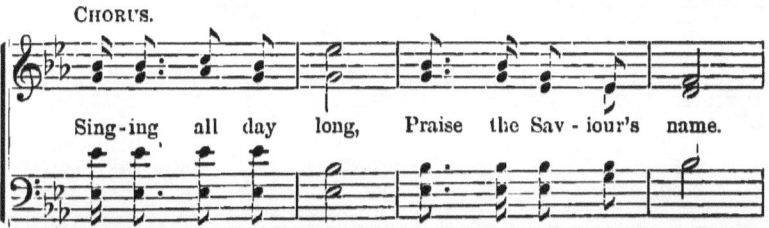

Sing-ing all day long, Praise the Sav-iour's name.

We are a band of happy, happy children, Singing all day long.

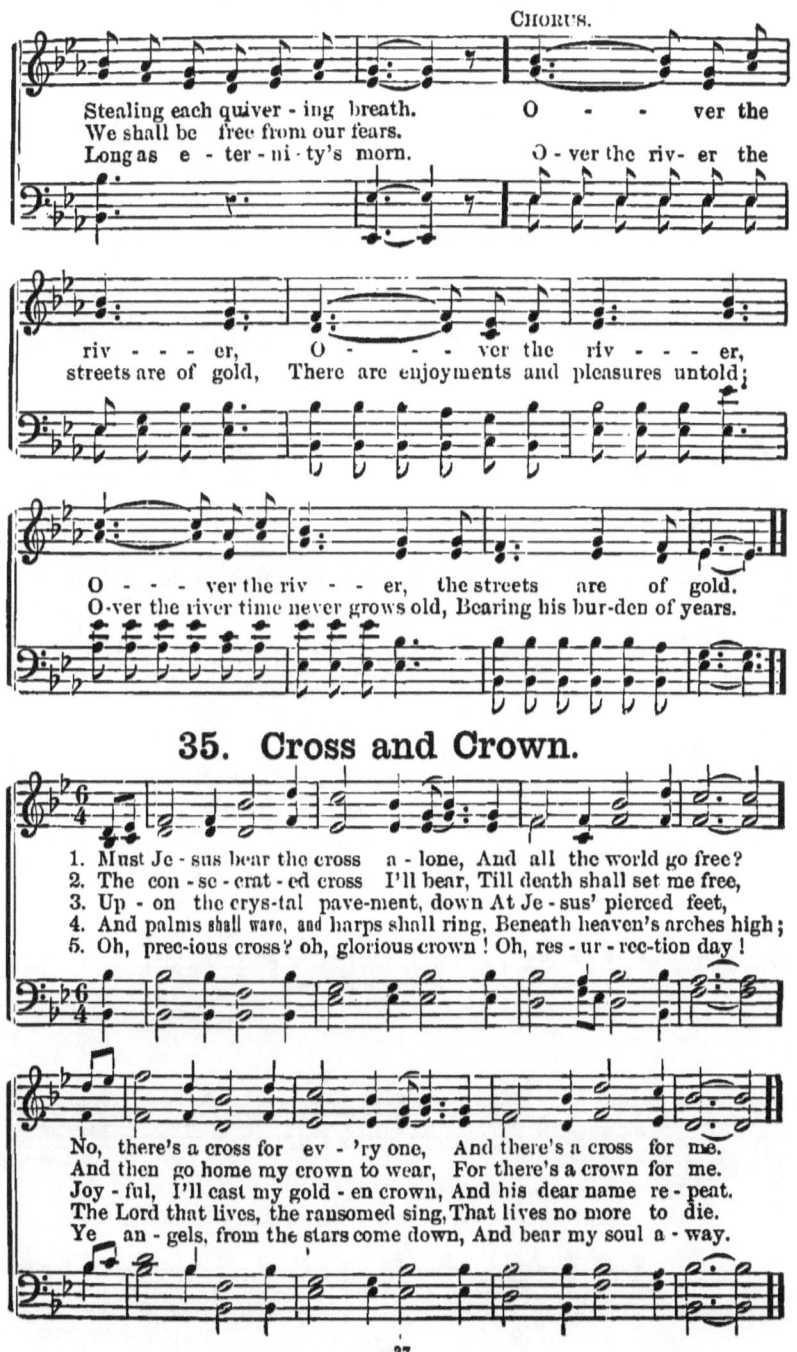

36. The Fountain of Life.

J. T. REESE.

1. There is a fountain filled with blood, Drawn from Immanuel's veins,
2. The dy-ing thief re-joiced to see That fountain in his day;
3. Thou dy-ing Lamb, Thy precious blood, Shall nev-er lose its power,

And sinners plunged beneath that flood, Lose all their guilt-y stains.
And there may I, tho' vile as he, Wash all my sins a-way.
Till all the ransomed church of God Be saved, to sin no more.

CHORUS.

The fount - ain is flow-ing, Come wash in its waters so free..........
The fountain of life is flow - ing, Come wash in its waters, its waters so free,

The fount - ain is flow - ing,
The fountain of life is flow - ing, Flow-ing for you and for me.

37. Calling Me Over the Tide.

JESSIE H. BROWN.   J. H. FILLMORE, by per.

1. Friends who have loved me are slip-ping a-way, Si-lent-ly on-ward they glide; Still are their voic-es, as backward they stray,
2. Dim-ly thro' gath-er-ing dark-ness I see Je-sus, my Friend and my Guide; An-gels are watching and waiting for me,
3. Nar-row the wa-ters, and tran-quil the shore; There my be-lov-ed a-bide,— Christ and the an-gels and friends gone be-fore,

REFRAIN.

Call-ing me o-ver the tide. Call-ing to me, they are calling to me, Loved ones are call-ing me o-ver the tide; They are call-ing to me, they are calling to me, Calling me o-ver the tide.

Copyright, 1886, by FILLMORE BROS.

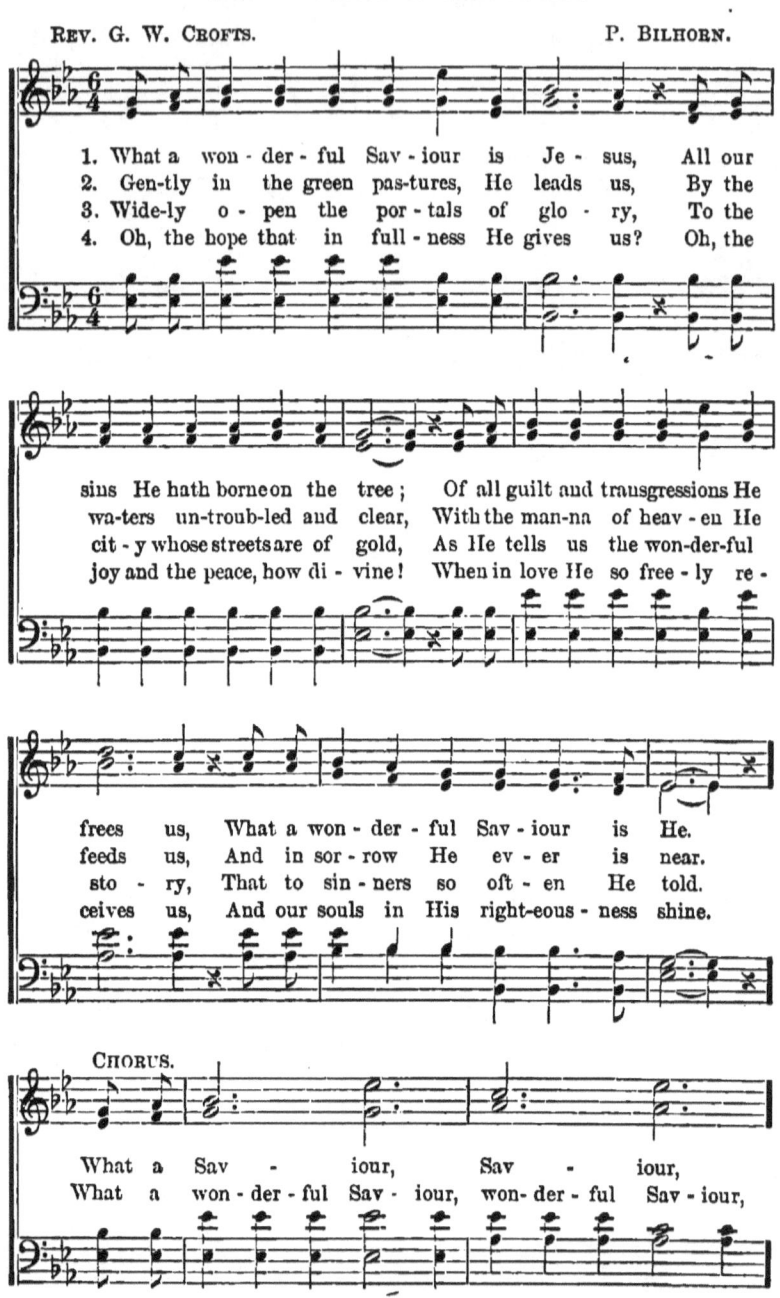

What a Saviour. Concluded.

Won-der-ful Sav-iour is Je-sus, What a Sav - iour,
What a won-der-ful Sav-iour,
Sav - iour, What a won-der-ful Sav-iour is He.
Won-der-ful Sav-iour,

39. Am I a Soldier of the Cross?

J. C. Lowry.

1. Am I a sol - dier of the cross, A fol-lower of the Lamb?
2. Must I be car - ried to the skies On flow-ery beds of ease,
3. Are there no foes for me to face? Must I not stem the flood?
4. Sure I must fight if I would reign: In-crease my cour-age, Lord;

And shall I fear to own his cause, Or blush to speak his name?
While oth - ers fought to win the prize, And sailed thro' blood-y seas?
Is this vile world a friend to grace, To help me on to God?
I'll bear the toil, in-dure the pain, Sup - port-ed by thy word.

5. Thy saints, in all this glorious war,
   Shall conquer, though they die;
   They see the triumph from afar,
   With Faith's discerning eye.

6. When that illustrious day shall rise
   And all thine armies shine,
   In robes of victory through the skies,
   The glory shall be thine.

40. The Open Gate.

"An entrance shall be administered unto you abundantyl."—Pet. i: 11.

Mrs. Lizzie Underwood.   S. C. Hanson.

1. I've heard them sing a-gain and a-gain, Of a gate that stands a-jar,
2. A wel-come home at the open gate, From a land of an-gels bright,
3. The sinner's friend, as he reaches down, With a Savior's wondrous love;

Of a sun-ny clime, and gold-en plain, And a sin-less land a-far,
Do these for the ransom'd spirits wait, As it gains the land of light?
Who prepares a mansion, robe, and crown, In his shin-ing courts a-bove,

But when I have past the chill-y tide, And en-ter my home a-bove;
We may not know of the joy un-told, The bliss of the oth-er side;
Will gather his flock in-to the fold, To the fold be-yond the tide;

I be-lieve the gate will o-pen wide, On its gold-en hinge of love.
But when I come to the gate of gold, I be-lieve 'twill o-pen wide.
As they near the gate, the gate of gold, I be-lieve 'twill o-pen wide.

The Open Gate—Concluded.

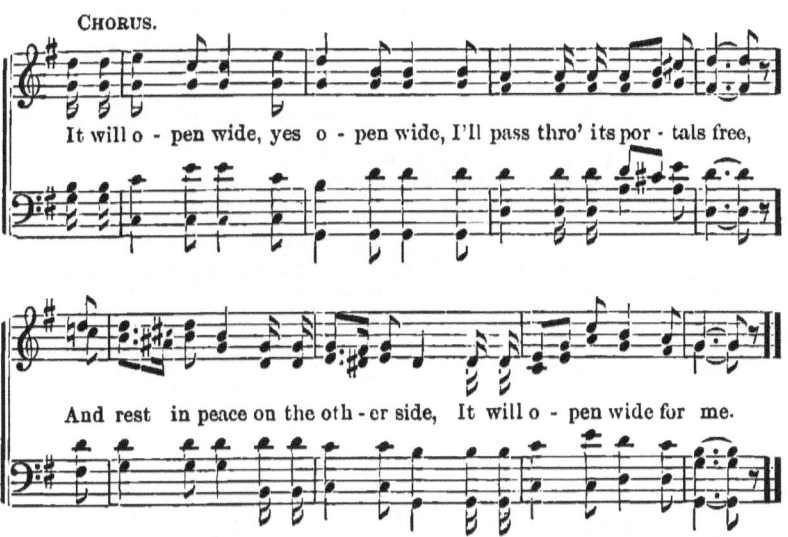

41. Jesus Lover of My Soul.

CHARLES WESLEY. S. B. MARSH.

2. Other refuge have I none,
   Hangs my helpless soul on Thee,
   Leave, oh leave me not alone,
   Still support and comfort me.
   All my trust on Thee is stayed,
   All my help from Thee I bring;
   Cover my defenseless head
   With the shadow of Thy wing.

3. Thou, O Christ, art all I want;
   More than all in Thee I find;
   Raise the fallen! cheer the faint!
   Heal the sick! and lead the blind!
   Just and holy is Thy name,
   I am all unrighteousness:
   Vile and full of sin I am,
   Thou art full of truth and grace.

42. I Know Not.

"Watch therefore: for ye know not what hour your Lord doth come." Matt. xxiv. 42.

JOHN McPHERSON.   J. F. KINSEY.

Duet, Ad lib.

1. I know not how soon God will call me, To leave all these scenes here be-low; Here tri-als and troub-les be-fall me, I care not how soon I may go.
2. To-night the death an-gel may whisper, The sum-mons for me to come home, And leave here a broth-er or sis-ter, My sud-den de-par-ture to mourn.
3. I know not how soon I'll be sing-ing, Sweet songs with the ran-somed up there; For-ev-er the an-thems are ringing, O'er heaven's dear land-scape so fair.

CHORUS.

I'm glad that I know not the coming Of Je-sus, my Master, my joy, But soon he will take me from roaming, To rest where no foes can annoy.

By per, "THE ECHO MUSIC CO."

44. Jesus Saves.

PRISCILLA J. OWENS. WM. J. KIRKPATRICK. By per.

1. We have heard a joy-ful sound, Je-sus saves, Je-sus saves;
2. Waft it on the roll-ing tide, Je-sus saves, Je-sus saves;
3. Sing a-bove the bat-tle's strife, Je-sus saves, Je-sus saves;
4. Give the winds a mighty voice, Je-sus saves, Je-sus saves;

Spread the glad-ness all a-round, Je-sus saves, Je-sus saves;
Tell to sin-ners, far and wide, Je-sus saves, Je-sus saves;
By His death and end-less life, Je-sus saves, Je-sus saves;
Let the na-tions now re-joice, Je-sus saves, Je-sus saves;

Bear the news to ev-'ry land, Climb the steeps and cross the waves,
Sing, ye is-lands of the sea, Ech-o back, ye o-cean caves,
Sing it soft-ly thro' the gloom, When the heart for mer-cy craves,
Shout sal-va-tion full and free, High-est hills and deep-est caves.

On-ward, 'tis our Lord's command, Je-sus saves, Je-sus saves.
Earth shall keep her Ju-bi-lee, Je-sus saves, Je-sus saves.
Sing in tri-umph o'er the tomb; Je-sus saves, Je-sus saves.
This our song of vic-to-ry, Je-sus saves, Je-sus saves.

Copyright, 1882, by JOHN J. HOOD.

45. Lead Me Safely On.

J. H. Leslie.   R. A. Glenn.

1. Lead me safe-ly on by the nar-row way, From the shores of time to the realms of day; By the cross of Christ may I ev-er stand, As I jour-ney on to the bet-ter land.
2. With a Shepherd's care, thro' the night and day, Keep me close to thee lest I go a-stray; Lead me safe-ly on, by thy ten-der love, Thro' this world of sin to my home a-bove.
3. Thro' the storms of life, 'mid the o-cean's foam, Lead me safe-ly on to my heav'nly home; At the fount of life, on the oth-er shore, Let me free-ly drink till I thirst no more.

REFRAIN.

Lead me on, lead me on, lead me on, By the strait and narrow way, Lead me on, lead me on, lead me on, lead me on, To the realms of end-less day.

Copyrighted. From "Purest Pearls."

46. Hosanna.

Unknown.   New Arrangement.

1. Thy worthiness is all our song, O Lamb of God, for Thou wast slain,
And by Thy blood brought'st us to God, Out of each nation, tribe and tongue.
2. Sal-va-tion to our God, who shines In face of Je-sus, on the throne,
The on - ly just and mer - ci - ful—Salvation to the worthy Lamb,
3. To Him who loved us, and hath washed Us from our sins in His own blood,
And who hath made us kings and priests To His own Father and His God,

To God hast made us kings and priests, And we shall reign up-on the earth:
With loud voice all the church ascribes; "Amen," say angels round the throne:
The glo - ry and do-min-ion be To Him e-ter-nal-ly. A-men.

CHORUS.

Ho-san-na! Ho-san-na! Ho - san na to the Lamb of God!

Glo - ry! glo - ry! let us sing Grate-ful prais-es to our King.

For You and For Me—Concluded.

Je-sus is call-ing, Calling, O sinner, come home.

49. Take Me as I Am.

CHARLOTTE ELLIOTT.
Melody by J. H. STOCKTON.
Har. by W. J. K.

1. Just as I am, with-out one plea, But that Thy blood was shed for me,
2. Just as I am, and wait-ing not To rid my soul of one dark blot—
3. Just as I am, tho' tossed a-bout, With many a conflict, many a doubt,
4. Just as I am, thou wilt receive, Wilt welcome, pardon, cleanse, relieve,
5. Just as I am—Thy love, unknown, Has broken ev- 'ry barrier down;

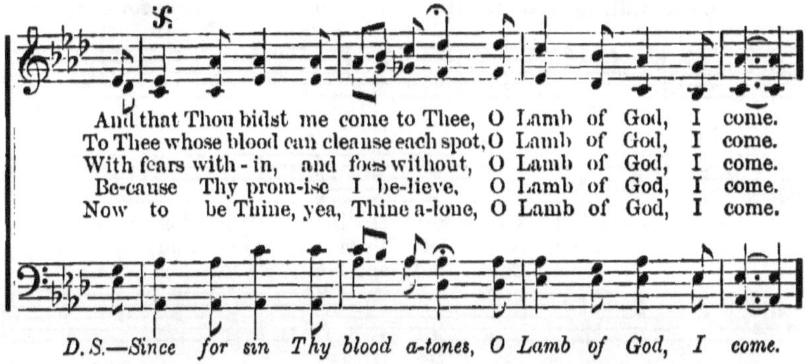

And that Thou bidst me come to Thee, O Lamb of God, I come.
To Thee whose blood can cleanse each spot, O Lamb of God, I come.
With fears with-in, and foes without, O Lamb of God, I come.
Be-cause Thy prom-ise I be-lieve, O Lamb of God, I come.
Now to be Thine, yea, Thine a-lone, O Lamb of God, I come.

D. S.—Since for sin Thy blood a-tones, O Lamb of God, I come.

REFRAIN.

Take me as I am,...... Take me as I am;...... And
Take me, take me as I am, Take me, take me as I am;

Come to the Savior To-Day—Concluded.

come, come,
come to the Sav-ior, Why will you lon-ger de-lay?

Come, come, come, come, *Repeat pp.*
Come to the Savior, come to the Savior, Come to the Savior to-day.

51. Come Unto Me.
LOWELL MASON.

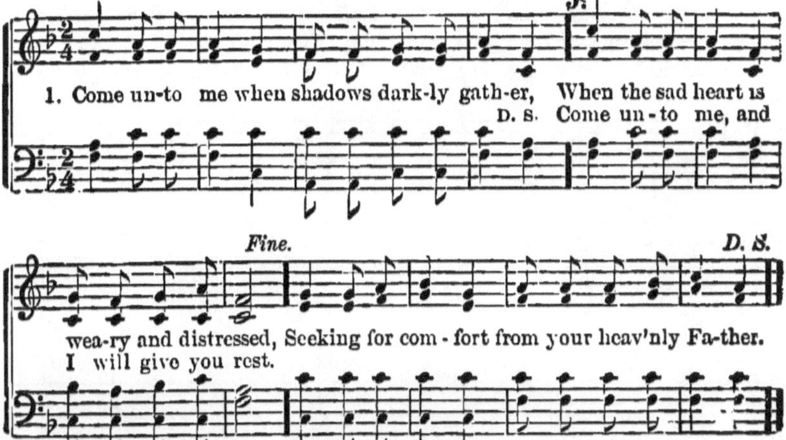

1. Come un-to me when shadows dark-ly gath-er, When the sad heart is
D. S. Come un-to me, and

Fine. D. S.
wea-ry and distressed, Seeking for com-fort from your heav'nly Fa-ther.
I will give you rest.

2. Ye who have mourned when the spring flowers were taken;
   When the ripe fruit fell richly to the ground;
   When the loved slept, in brighter homes to waken,
   Where their pale brows with spirit-wreaths are crowned.

3. Large are the mansions in your Father's dwelling,
   Glad are homes that sorrows never dim;
   Sweet are the harps in holy music swelling,
   Soft are the tones which raise the heavenly hymn.

4. There, like an Eden, blossoming in gladness,
   Bloom the fair flowers the earth too rudely pressed:
   Come unto me, all ye who droop in sadness,
   Come unto me, and I will give you rest.

We Answer the Call--Continued.

We Answer the Call.—Concluded.

53. Shout the Tidings.

1. Shout the tidings of salvation, To the aged and the young;
2. Shout the tidings of salvation, O'er the prairies of the West,
3. Shout the tidings of salvation, Mingling with the ocean's roar,
4. Shout the tidings of salvation, O'er the islands of the sea,

Till the precious invitation Waken ev'ry heart and tongue.
Till each gath'ring congregation With the gospel sound is blest.
Till the ships of ev'ry nation Bear the news from shore to shore.
Till, in humble adoration, All to Christ shall bow the knee.

CHORUS.

Send the sound the earth around, From the rising to the settings of the sun,

Till each gath'ring crowd shall proclaim aloud, The glorious work is done.

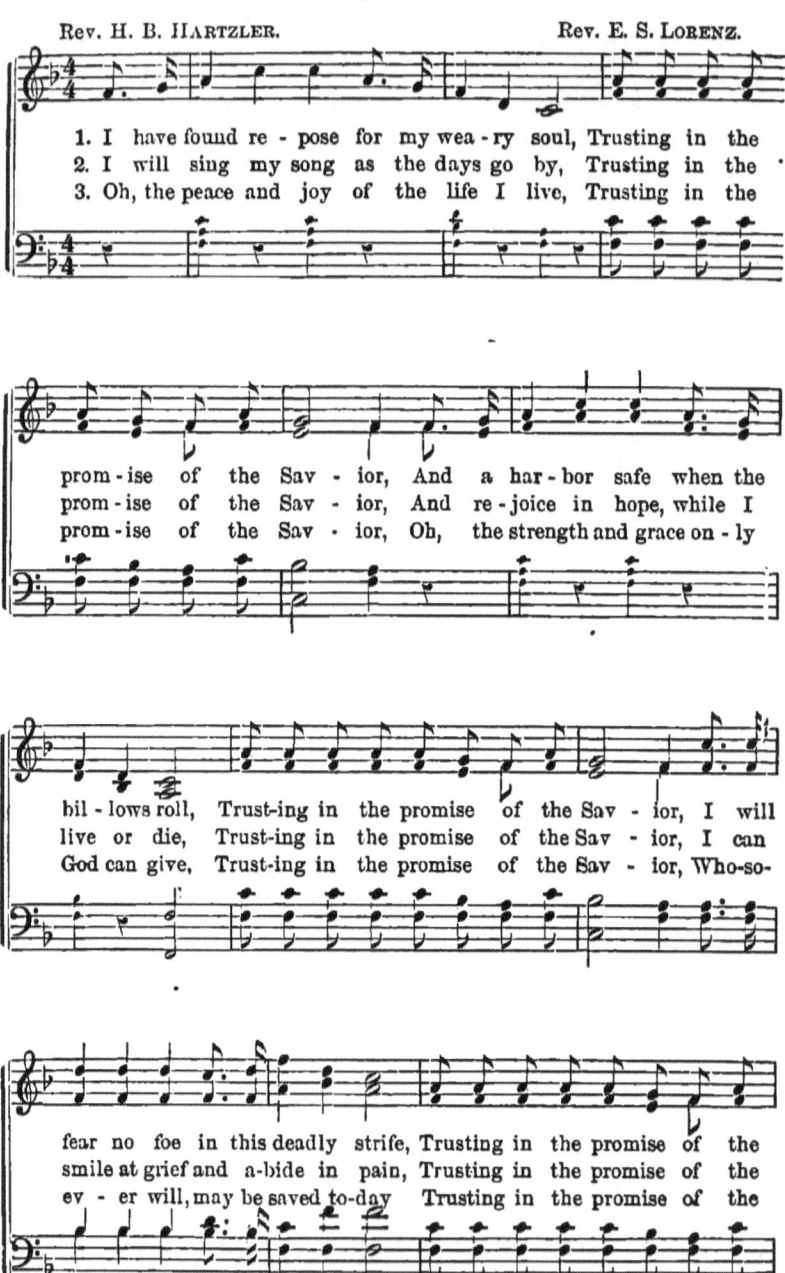

Trusting in the Promise—Concluded.

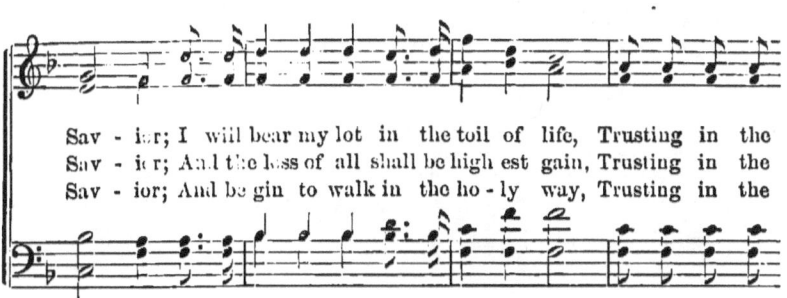

Sav - ior; I will bear my lot in the toil of life, Trusting in the
Sav - ior; And the loss of all shall be highest gain, Trusting in the
Sav - ior; And begin to walk in the ho - ly way, Trusting in the

REFRAIN.

prom-ise of the Sav - ior. Rest-ing on His mighty arm for-

ev - er, Nev - er from His lov-ing heart to sev - er, I will rest by

grace, In His strong embrace, Trusting in the promise of the Sav - ior.

Who is on the Lord's Side—Concluded.

help - - - er; Oth - er souls to bring?
Who will be his help-er, Oth-er souls to bring? Oth-er souls to bring?

56. All Hail the Power of Jesus' Name.

PERONET. OLIVER HOLDEN

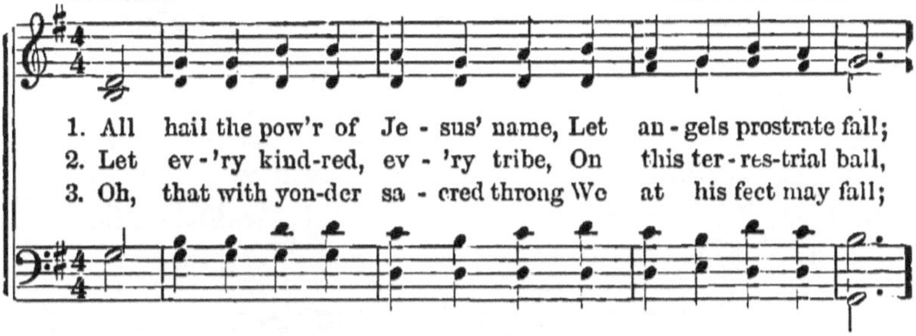

1. All hail the pow'r of Je-sus' name, Let an-gels prostrate fall;
2. Let ev-'ry kind-red, ev-'ry tribe, On this ter-res-trial ball,
3. Oh, that with yon-der sa-cred throng We at his feet may fall;

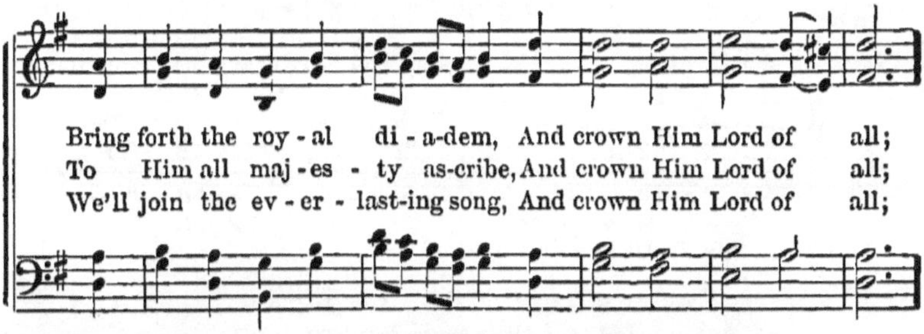

Bring forth the roy-al di-a-dem, And crown Him Lord of all;
To Him all maj-es-ty as-cribe, And crown Him Lord of all;
We'll join the ev-er-last-ing song, And crown Him Lord of all;

Bring forth the roy-al di-a-dem, And crown Him Lord of all.
To Him all maj-es-ty as-cribe, And crown Him Lord of all.
We'll join the ev-er-last-ing song; And crown Him Lord of all.

57. Joy to the World.

ISAAC WATTS.   HANDEL.

1. Joy to the world, the Lord is come! Let earth re-ceive her King;

Let ev-'ry heart prepare Him room, And heav'n and nature sing, And
And heav'n and nature
And heav'n and nature

heav'n and nature sing, And heav'n, And heav'n and na-ture sing.
sing,
sing, And heav'n and nature sing,

2. Joy to the earth, the Savior reigns!
   Let men their songs employ;
   While fields and floods, rocks, hills and plains,
   Repeat the sounding joy.

3. No more let sins and sorrows grow,
   Nor thorns infest the ground;
   He comes to make His blessings flow,
   Far as the curse is found.

4. He rules the world with truth and grace,
   And makes the nations prove
   The glories of His righteousness,
   And wonders of His love.

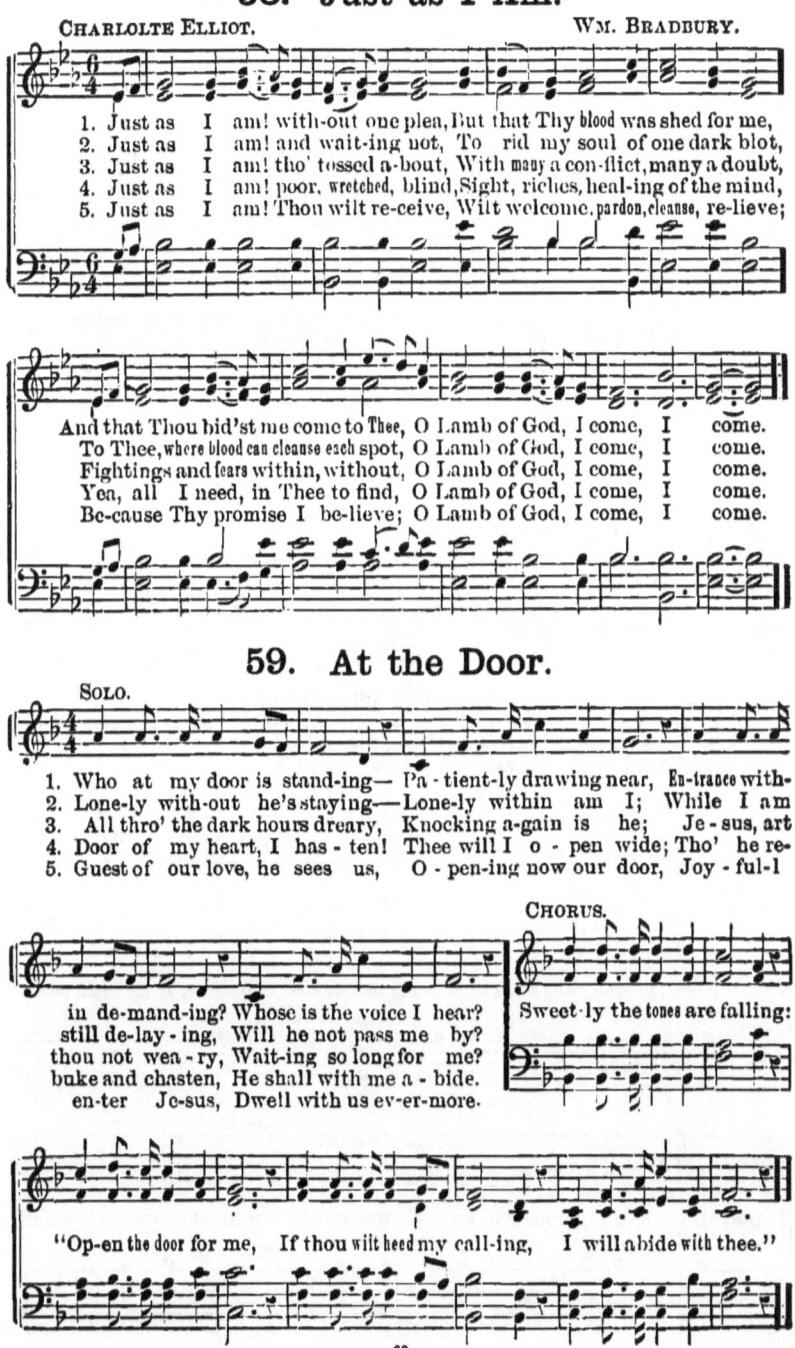

60. The Angels' Welcome.

L. H. Jameson.   Arr. by J. V. Coombs, as sung by L. H. Jameson.

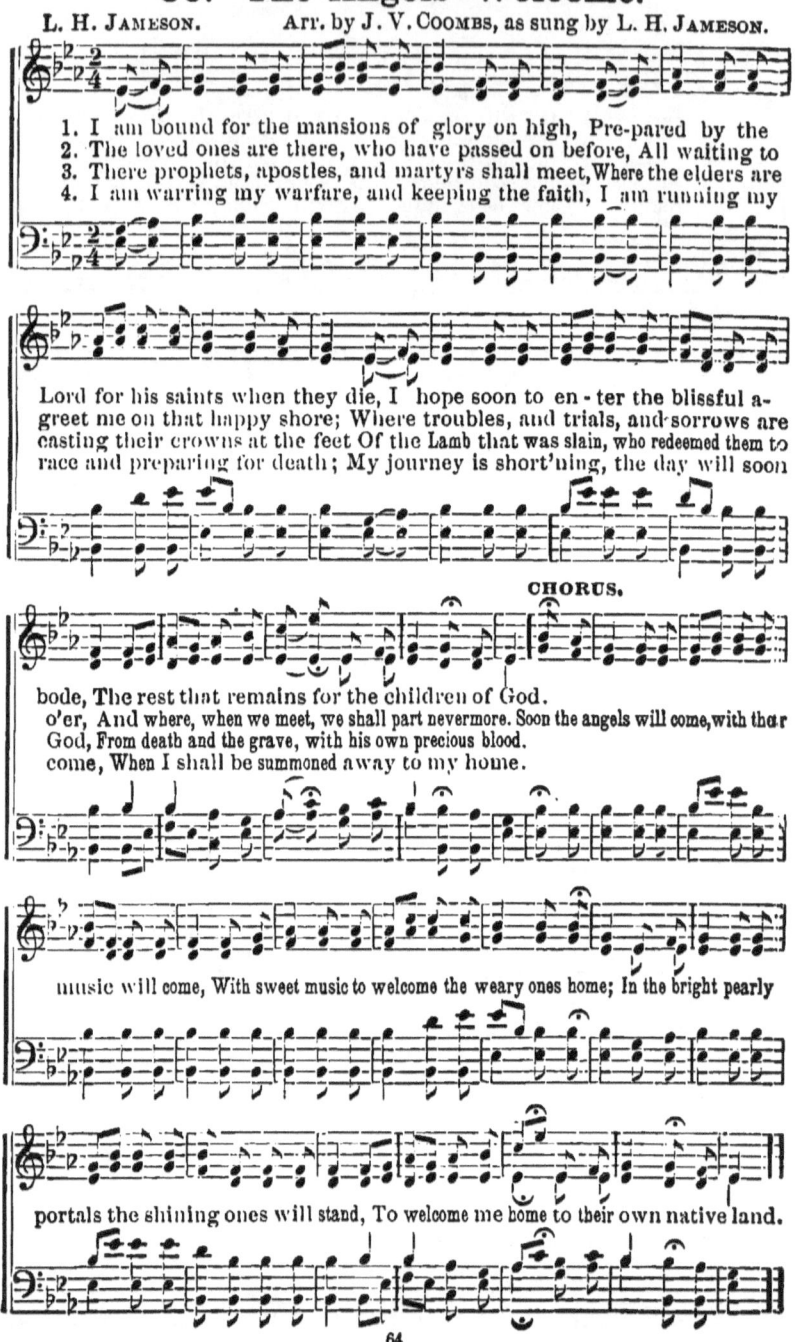

1. I am bound for the mansions of glory on high, Pre-pared by the Lord for his saints when they die, I hope soon to en-ter the blissful a-bode, The rest that remains for the children of God.
2. The loved ones are there, who have passed on before, All waiting to greet me on that happy shore; Where troubles, and trials, and sorrows are o'er, And where, when we meet, we shall part nevermore.
3. There prophets, apostles, and martyrs shall meet, Where the elders are casting their crowns at the feet Of the Lamb that was slain, who redeemed them to God, From death and the grave, with his own precious blood.
4. I am warring my warfare, and keeping the faith, I am running my race and preparing for death; My journey is short'ning, the day will soon come, When I shall be summoned away to my home.

CHORUS.

Soon the angels will come, with their music will come, With sweet music to welcome the weary ones home; In the bright pearly portals the shining ones will stand, To welcome me home to their own native land.

62. In the Shadow of the Rock.

Arr. by J. V. Coombs. Arr. by J. T. Reese.

Solo or duet.

1. In a drear-y land I wander, And with falt'ring steps I walk; But I'll
2. Let me go where my Redeemer Has prepared for me sweet rest; In the
3. So with patient faith I'll wander, And with loving heart I'll walk; I will
4. Let me go, my soul is weary Of the chains which rudely mock; I'll be

CHORUS.

soon be resting yonder In the shadow of the rock.
golden home up yonder, To the mansions of the blest.
soon be resting yonder, In the shadow of the rock.
resting over yonder In the shadow of the rock.

In the shadow of the rock, In the shadow of the rock; I will soon be resting yonder, In the shadow of the rock.

63. Consecration.

F. R. Havergal. From Mozart.

1. Take my life, and let it be Con-se-cra-ted, Lord to Thee;
2. Take my hands, and let them move At the im-pulse of Thy love;
3. Take my voice, and let me sing Al-ways, on-ly for my King;
4. Take my sil-ver and my gold; Not a mite would I with-hold;
5. Take my will, and make it Thine; It shall be no lon-ger mine;
6. Take my love—my Lord, I pour, At Thy feet its treasure store;

Take my moments and my days, Let them flow in cease-less praise.
Take my feet, and let them be Swift and beau-ti-ful for Thee.
Take my lips, and let them be Filled with mes-sa-ges for Thee.
Take my in-tel-lect, and use Ev-'ry power as Thou shalt choose.
Take my heart—it is Thine own; It shall be Thy roy-al Throne.
Take my-self, and I will be Ev-er, on-ly, all for Thee.

64. Tarry with Me.

Mrs. C. S. Smith.   Knowles Shaw.

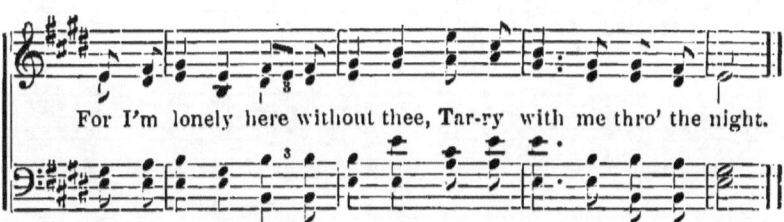

2 Many friends were gathered round me,
In the bright days of the past;
But the grave has closed above them,
And I linger here the last.

3 Deeper, deeper grow the shadows,
Paler now the glowing west,

Swift the night of death advances;
Shall it be the night of rest?

4 Tarry with me, oh, my Savior,
Lay my head upon thy breast
Till the morning; then awake me,
Morning of eternal rest.

65. There is a Fountain.

WM. COWPER.   AMERICAN MELODY.

2 O Lamb of God! thy precious blood
  Shall never lose its power,
Till all the ransomed church of God
  Are saved, to sin no more.

3 Ere since by faith I saw the stream
  Thy flowing wounds supply,

Redeeming love has been my theme,
  And shall be till I die.

4 And when this lisping, stammering tongue
  Lies silent in the grave,
Then, in a nobler, sweeter song,
  I'll sing thy power to save.

66. Jesus Died for You.

ISAAC WATTS.   S. J. VAIL.

2 Was it for crimes that I had done
  He groaned upon the tree?
Amazing pity! grace unknown!
  And love beyond degree!—CHO.

3 Well might the sun in darkness hide,
  And shut his glories in,
When God's own Son was crucified
  For man, the creature's sin.—CHO.

4 Thus might I hide my blushing face
  While his dear cross appears.
Dissolve my heart in thankfulness,
  And melt mine eyes to tears.—CHO.

5 But drops of grief can ne'er repay
  The debt of love I owe:
Here, Lord, I give myself away—
  'Tis all that I can do.—CHO.

67. Waiting.

Geo. F. Hall.   Mrs. Laura Hall.

1. I am waiting, simply waiting, While the hours are speeding by,
2. I am waiting, simply waiting, For that gold-en morn to dawn,
3. Yes I'm waiting, simply waiting, As I feel the time draws nigh,

For the com-ing of my Savior, Who for me did deign to die.
When I'll meet my precious loved ones, Who be-fore me long have gone.
When all tongues shall speak the praises, Of our Lord enthroned on high.

He is com-ing, shortly coming, Back to earth where he was slain,
Oh! my soul is filled with longing, As I tar - ry here a - lone,
And I'm sing-ing while I'm waiting, For my heart is full of joy.

Refrain. O I'm waiting, simply waiting, While the hours are speeding by,

To re-ceive his faithful servants, Who with him shall ev-er reign.
Longing for the bliss of heaven, Long-ing for that hap- py home.
Praise the Lord, O praise him ever; Let all men his praise employ.

Wait-ing for my com-ing Savior, Who for me did deign to die.

70. Under the Cross.

CHAS. WESLEY.   E. O. EXCELL.

1. Je-sus Lov-er of my soul, Let me to Thy bo-som fly,
2. Hide me, O my Saviour, hide, Till the storm of life is past;
3. Oth-er ref-uge have I none, Hangs my helpless soul on Thee,
4. All my trust on Thee is stayed, All my help from Thee I bring;

While the near-er wa-ters roll, While the tempest still is high!
Safe in-to the ha-ven guide, O receive my soul at last!
Leave, O leave me not a-lone, Still support and comfort me;
Cov-er my de-fence-less head With the shadow of Thy wing!

Hal-le-lu-jah!

CHORUS.

Un-der the cross I lay my sins, Un-der the cross they lie;
Un-der the cross I lay my sins, Un-der the cross I'll die.

5. Plenteous grace with Thee is found,
    Grace to cover all my sin;
    Let the healing streams abound;
    Make and keep me pure within.

6. Thou of life the fountain art,
    Freely let me take of Thee:
    Spring Thou up within my heart,
    Rise to all eternity.

Copyright, 1889, by E. O. Excell.

71. Lo, I Am with You.

Mrs. J. V. C.   Mat. xxviii, 20.   Mrs. J. V. COOMBS.

1. Hear the words of long a-go, From the mount in Gal-i-lee,
2. See the heath-en na-tions bow, As they catch the ray of light,
3. Loud and strong the cry comes on To us as to those of old,

Spok-en by the Lord of Love "Teach the world to fol-low me."
Eag-er now to be released From the dark-ness of the night.
"Teach the world to fol-low me," Let the Sto-ry oft be told.

Lo! I am with you, Lo! I am with you,
Lo! I am with you al-ways ev-en to the end.

72. Sweet By-and-By,

1 There's a land that is fairer than day
And by faith we can see it afar;
For the Father waits over the way,
To prepare us a dwelling-place there.

CHO.—In the sweet by-and-by,
We shall meet on that beautiful shore;
In the sweet by-and-by,
We shall meet on that beautiful shore.

2 We shall meet on that beautiful shore
The melodious songs of the blest;
And our spirits shall sorrow no more—
Not a sigh for the blessing of rest.

3 To our bountiful Father above
We will offer the tribute of praise,
For the glorious gifts of his love,
And the blessidgs that hallow our days.

73. Sound the Battle Cry.

74. Communion.

J. V. C. J. V. COOMBS.

1. We come this sacred day O Lord, To worship at thy feet; Oh, guide and
2. This Lord's Day morn we come to pray, To read thy holy word, Oh, keep us
3. A few more days for us to roam, A few more meetings blest. And God will

keep us by thy word, As we commune with Thee, As we commune with Thee.
in the good old way, And take us home to God, And take us home to God.
call his children home, To be with Christ at rest, To be with Christ at rest.

75. Asleep in Jesus.

Mrs. M. MACKAY. BRADBURY.

1. Asleep in Jesus! Blessed sleep, From which none ever wakes to weep;
2. Asleep in Je - sus! O how sweet To be for such a slumber meet;
3. Asleep in Je - sus! O for me May such a bliss-ful refuge be!

A calm and un-dis-turbed re-pose, Unbroken by the last of foes!
With ho-ly con - fi - dence to sing, That death has lost its venomed sting!
Securely shall my ash-es lie, And wait the summons from on high.

76. Seeking the Lost.

W. A. OGDEN.

1. Seek-ing the lost, yes, kind-ly en-treat-ing Wan-der-ers on the mountain a-stray; "Come un-to me," His message re-peat-ing, Words of the Mas-ter speaking to-day.
2. Seek-ing the lost, and point-ing to Je-sus, Souls that are weak, and hearts that are sore; Leading them forth in ways of sal-va-tion, Show-ing the path to life ev-er-more.
3. Thus I would go on missions of mer-cy, Fol-low-ing Christ from day un-to day; Cheering the faint, and rais-ing the fall-en; Pointing the lost to Je-sus the way.

CHORUS.

Going a-far up-on the mountain,
Going a-far............ up-on the mount-ain, Bringing the

By per. of W. A. Ogden, Toledo, Ohio.

Seeking the Lost—Concluded.

Bringing the wan-d'rer back a-gain, back a-gain.
wan - - - - d'rer back a - gain..........

In-to the fold of my Re-deem-er,
In-to the fold.......... of my Re-deem - er,.......... Jesus, the

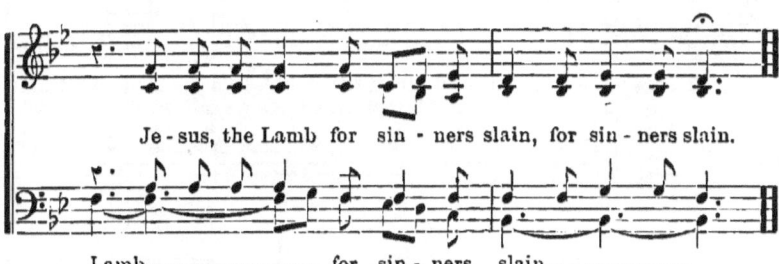

Je-sus, the Lamb for sin-ners slain, for sin-ners slain.
Lamb.................... for sin - ners slain..............

77. Doxology.

Praise God, from whom all blessings flow;
Praise him, all creatures here below;
Praise him above, ye heavenly host;
Praise Father, Son and Holy Ghost.

78. The Great Physician.

1 The great Physician now is near,
   The sympathizing Jesus;
He speaks the drooping heart to cheer,
   Oh, hear the voice of Jesus.

Cho.—Sweetest note in seraph song,
   Sweetest name on mortal tongue,
   Sweetest carol ever sung,
   Jesus, blessed Jesus.

2 All glory to the dying Lamb!
   I now believe in Jesus;
I love the blessed Savior's name,
   I love the name of Jesus.

3 His name dispels my guilt and fear,
   No other name but Jesus;
Oh, how my soul delights to hear
   The precious name of Jesus.

4 And when to that bright world above,
   We rise to see our Jesus,
We'll sing around the throne of love,
   His name, the name of Jesus.

The Sinner and the Song—Concluded.

80. Deliverance will Come.

J. B. M.   Rev. Jno. B. Matthias.

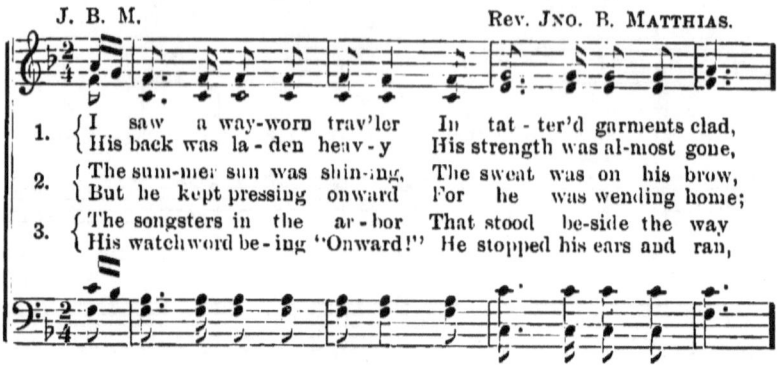

1. I saw a way-worn trav'ler   In tat-ter'd garments clad,
   His back was la-den heav-y   His strength was al-most gone,
2. The sum-mer sun was shin-ing,   The sweat was on his brow,
   But he kept pressing onward   For he was wending home;
3. The songsters in the ar-bor   That stood be-side the way
   His watchword be-ing "Onward!"   He stopped his ears and ran,

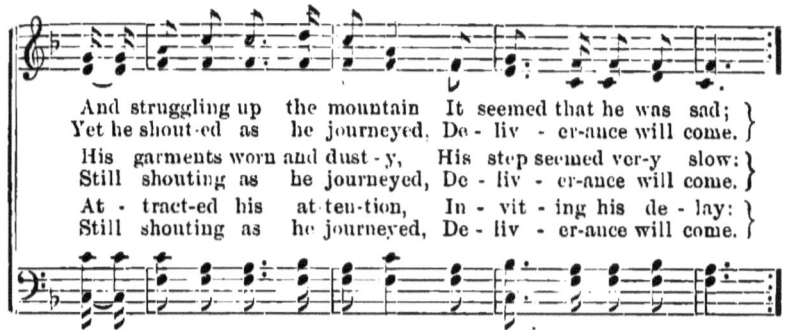

And struggling up the mountain   It seemed that he was sad;
Yet he shout-ed as he journeyed,   De-liv-er-ance will come.
His garments worn and dust-y,   His step seemed ver-y slow;
Still shouting as he journeyed,   De-liv-er-ance will come.
At-tract-ed his at-ten-tion,   In-vit-ing his de-lay;
Still shouting as he journeyed,   De-liv-er-ance will come.

CHORUS.

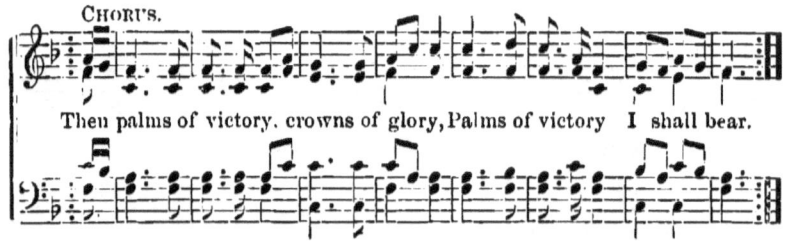

Then palms of victory, crowns of glory, Palms of victory I shall bear.

I saw him in the evening,
  The sun was bending low,
He'd overtopped the mountain,
  And reached the vale below:
He saw the golden city,—
  His everlasting home,—
And shouted loud, Hosanna,
  Deliverance will come!

5 While gazing on that city,
  Just o'er the narrow flood,
A band of holy angels
  Came from the throne of God:

They bore him on their pinions'
  Safe o'er the dashing foam;
And joined him in his triumph,—
  Deliverance had come!

6 I heard the song of triumph
  They sang upon that shore,
Saying, Jesus has redeemed us
  To suffer nevermore:
Then, casting his eyes backward
  On the race which he had run,
He shouted loud, Hosanna,
  Deliverance has come!

81. My Ain Countrie

Miss M. A. LEE. Scotch Song. Arr.

2. I've his good word of promise, that some gladsome day the King
To his ain royal palace, his banished, hame will bring,
Wi' eyes, an' wi' heart running owre we shall see
"The King in his beauty," an' our ain countrie,
My sins have been many, and my sorrows have been sair;
But there they'll never vex me, nor be remembered mair.
For his blood hath made me white, and his hand shall dry my e'e,
When he brings me hame at last to my ain countrie.

3. He is faithfu' that hath promised, an' he'll surely come again,
He'll keep his trust wi' me, at what hour I dinna ken;
But he bids me still to wait, an' ready aye to be,
To go at any moment to my ain countrie.
So I'm watching aye, and singing o' my hame as I wait,
For the soun'ing o' his footfa' this side the gowden gate,
God gives his grace to each ane wha listens noo to me,
That we all may go in gladness to our ain countrie.

Tell it Again—Concluded.

of men, "No-bod-y ev-er has told me be-fore!"

83. Come Home To-Night.

J. V. C. J. V. COOMBS.

1. Be-hold what love the Sav-ior gave To sinners who had gone astray,
2. That love abounds, 'tis of-fered thee If you confess he is the Lord,
3. Your stay will be more joy-ous here, By trusting in his ho-ly love,
4. Oh, come to-day, Oh, why de-lay, For mansions are prepared for thee,

Ac-cept that love, confess his name, Oh, wand'rer will you come to-day?
His blood was shed on Cal - va - ry, Oh, will you not believe his word?
Live by his word and learn of him, And thus receive a home a-bove.
A robe and crown at his right hand. Oh, wand'rer will you not be free?

CHORUS.

Come home to-night, come home to-night, The spirit and the bride say come,

Come home to-night, come home to-night, Oh, sinner will you come to-night?

85. Christ is Precious.

ELIZA SHERMAN.   J. H. FILLMORE.

1. Oh, the precious love of Je - sus, Grow-ing sweeter day by day,
2. But we cannot know the full-ness Of the Savior's wondrous love,
3. Come and taste the love of Je - sus, At his feet thy burdens lay;

Tun - ing all my heart so joy - ous To a heav'nly mel-o - dy.
Till we see and know his glo - ry, In the heav'nly home above.
Trust him with thy grief and sorrow, Bear this joy-ful song a - way.

CHORUS.

Christ is precious, Christ is precious, In life's journey he will lead thee;

Christ is precious, Christ is precious, He will lead thee all the way.

86. Work, for the night is coming.

1 Work, for the night is coming,
   Work through the morning hours;
   Work while the dew is sparkling,
   Work 'mid springing flow'rs;
   Work when the day grows brighter,
   Work in the glowing sun;
   Work, for the night is coming,
   When man's work is done.

2 Work, for the night is coming,
   Work through the sunny noon;
   Fill brightest hours with labor,
   Rest comes sure and soon.
   Give every flying moment
   Something to keep in store;
   Work, for the night is coming,
   When man works no more.

87. The Model Church.

Arr. by J. V. Coombs.

1. Well, wife, I've found the model church, And worshipp'd here to day; It made me think of good old times. Before my hair was gray, The meeting house was fin-er built, Than they were years a-go, But then I found when I went in. It was not built for show.

2. The sex-ton did not set me down, A-way back by the door; He knew that I was old and deaf, And saw that I was poor, He must have been a christian man, He led me bold-ly thro' The long aisle of that crowded church, To find a pleasant pew.

3. I wish you'd heard the singing, wife, It had the old-time ring; The preach-er said with trumpet voice, Let all the peo-ple sing. "Old Cor-o-na-tion," was the tune, The mu-sic upward roll'd, Till I tho't I heard the an-gel-choir Strike all the harps of gold.

4 My deafness seemed to melt away,
My spirit caught the fire;
I joined their feeble, trembling voice,
With that melodious choir;
And sang, as in my youthful days,
"Let angel's prostrate fall;
Bring forth the roy-al di-a-dem,
And crown him Lord of all.

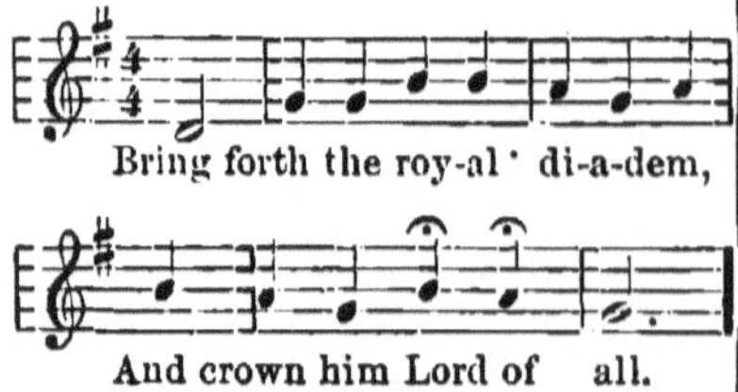

5 I tell you, wife, it did me good
To sing that hymn once more;
I felt like some wrecked mariner
Who gets a glimpse of shore.
I almost want to lay aside
This weather-beaten form,
And anchor in the blessed port,
Forever from the storm.

6 'Twas not a flowery sermon, wife,
But simple gospel truth;
It fitted humble men like me;
It suited hopeful youth,
To win immortal souls to Christ,
The earnest preacher tried;
He talked not of himself or creed,
But Jesus crucified.

The Model Church—Concluded.

7 Dear wife, the toil will soon be o'er,
  The victory soon be won.
  The shining land is just ahead,
  Our race is nearly run,
  We're nearing Canaan's happy shore,
  Our home so bright and fair;
  Thank God, we'll never sin again;

There'll be no sorrow there; There'll be no sorrow there. In heaven a-bove where all is love

88. No Sorrow There.

1. Je-ru-sa-lem, my hap-py home, O how I long for thee!
2. Thy walls are all of precious stones, Most glorious to be-hold!
3. Thy gar-dens and thy pleasant greens My stud-y long have been;
4. If heav-en be thus glorious, Lord, Why should I stay from thence?
5. Reach down, reach down Thine arms of grace, And cause me to as-cend

When will my sor-rows have an end? Thy joys, when shall I see?
Thy gates are rich-ly set with pearl, Thy streets are paved with gold.
Such sparkling gems by hu-man sight Have nev-er yet been seen.
What fol-ly 'tis that I should dread To die and go from hence!
Where con-gre-ga-tions ne'er break up, And joy shall nev-er end.

D. S. *In heaven a-bove where all is love There'll be no sor-row there.*

CHORUS D. S.

There'll be no sor-row there, There'll be no sor-row there,

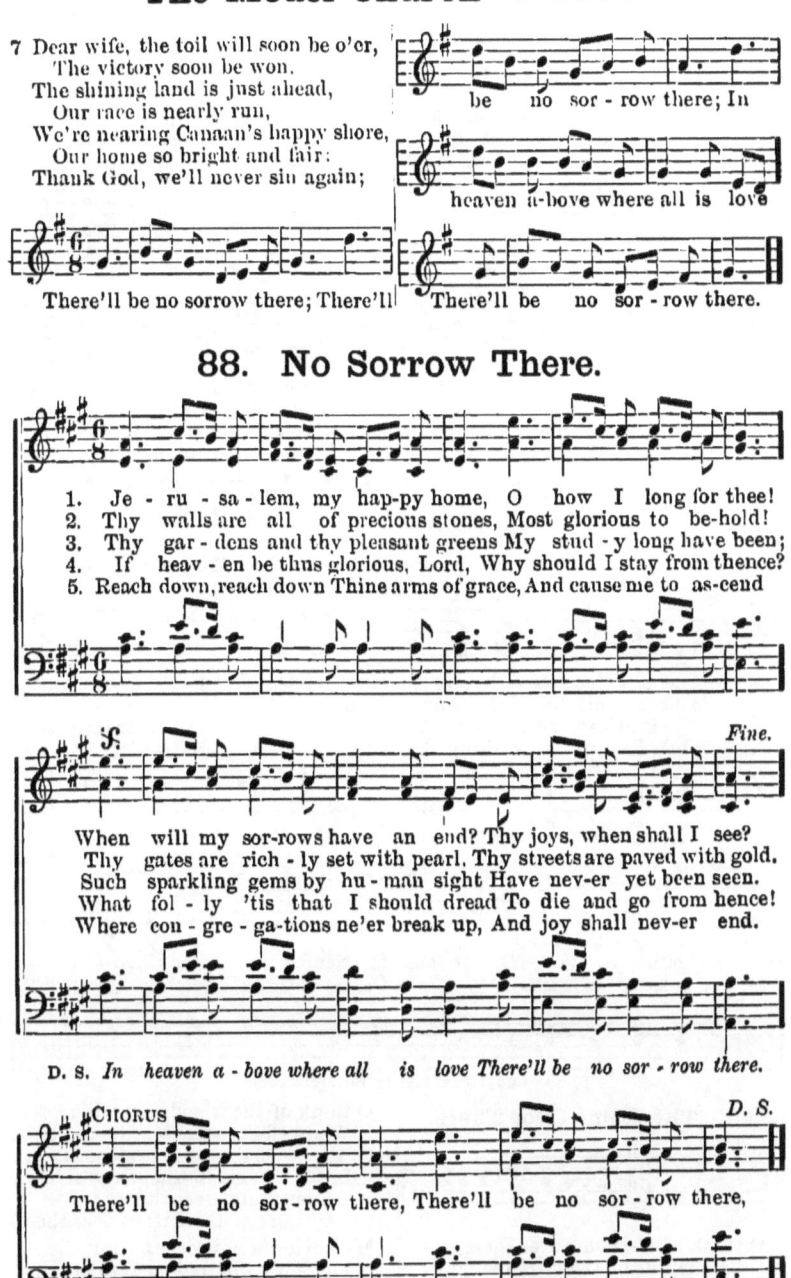

89. Jesus is Coming Again.

J. H. P.   J. H. PAINTER.

1. O I wonder when Jesus is coming again His waiting believers to bless; And gather to heaven his faithful ones, then, And give them sweet heavenly rest?
2. O when will the angels their shouting begin, When Jesus our Savior will come, To conquer forever the kingdom of sin, And take all his chosen ones home?
3. Many loved ones will meet us and cheer our glad souls, Our joys will be full then, I know; Hallelujahs will ring when we enter the goal, O Christian, be ready to go!
4. O sinner, delay not, the time is too near, It may be e'en now at your door; O come to the Savior, there's nothing to fear, While Jesus is walking before!

D. S.— O brother, rejoice! for the promise is sure, Yes, Jesus is coming again.

CHORUS.

O, Jesus is coming again! O, Jesus is coming again! O, Jesus is coming again!

Copyright, 1884 by Fillmore Bros.

90. The Home Over There.

1 O think of the home over there,
By the side of the river of light,
Where the saints, all immortal and fair,
Are robed in their garments of white,
Over there, over there,
O think of the home over there,

2 O think of the friends over there,
Who before us the journey have trod,
Of the songs that they breathe on the air,
In their home in the palace of God,
Over there, over there,
O think of the friends over there.

3 My Savior is now over there;
There my kindred and friends are at rest;
Then away from my sorrow and care,
Let me fly to the land of the blest.
Over there, over there,
My Savior is now over there.

91. My Country, 'tis of Thee.

S. F. SMITH. (AMERICA.)

1. My country, 'tis of thee, Sweet land of liberty, Of thee I sing; Land where my
2. My native country, thee, Land of the noble free, Thy name I love; I love thy
3. Let music swell the breeze, And ring from all the trees Sweet freedom's song; Let mortal
4. Our fathers' God, to Thee, Author of liberty, To Thee we sing; Long may our

cres.

fathers died, Land of the Pilgrims' pride, From ev'ry mountain side, Let freedom ring.
rocks and rills, Thy woods and templed hills, My heart with rapture thrills Like that a-bove.
tongues awake, Let all that breathe partake, Let rocks their silence break, The sound prolong.
land be bright, With freedom's holy light, Protect us by Thy might, Great God, our King!

92. I Am Coming to the Cross.

WM. MCDONALD. WM. G. FISHER.

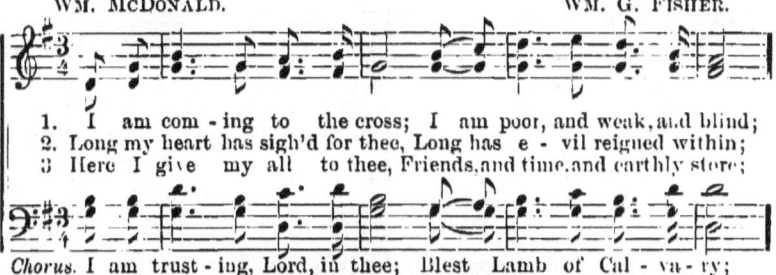

1. I am com-ing to the cross; I am poor, and weak, and blind;
2. Long my heart has sigh'd for thee, Long has e-vil reigned within;
3. Here I give my all to thee, Friends, and time, and earthly store;

Chorus. I am trust-ing, Lord, in thee; Blest Lamb of Cal-va-ry;

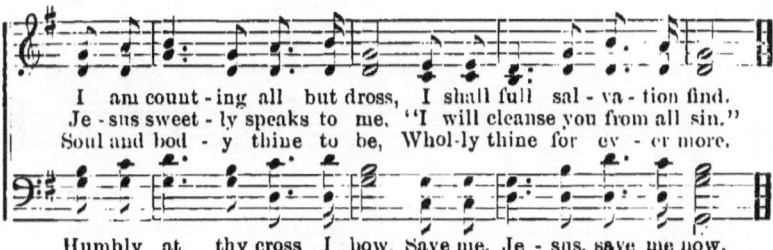

I am count-ing all but dross, I shall full sal-va-tion find.
Je-sus sweet-ly speaks to me, "I will cleanse you from all sin."
Soul and bod-y thine to be, Whol-ly thine for ev-er more.

Humbly at thy cross I bow, Save me, Je-sus, save me now.

95. Flee as a Bird.

96. The Handwriting on the Wall.

K. SHAW. KNOWLES SHAW, by per.

1. At the feast of Bel-shaz-zar and a thousand of his lords,
2. See the brave captive Daniel as he stood be-fore the throng,
3. See the faith, zeal, and courage that would dare to do the right.
4. So our deeds are re-cord-ed, there's a Hand that's writing now;

While they drank from gol'den ves-sels, as the book of truth records,
And rebuked the haughty monarch for his might - y deeds of wrong;
Which the Spir - it gave to Dan-iel, this the se - cret of his might;
Sin-ner, give your heart to Je-sus, to his roy - al mandate bow;

In the night as they rev-el in the roy - al pal-ace hall,
As he read out the writing—'twas the doom of one and all,
In his home in Ju - de - a, or a cap-tive in the hall,
For the day is approaching, it must come to one and all,

They were seized with consternation, 'twas the hand up-on the wall.
For the kingdom now was finished, said the hand ap-on the wall.
He un-der-stood the writing of his God up on the wall.
When the sinner's con-dem-na-tion will be writ - ten on the wall.

CHORUS.

'Tis the hand of God on the wall; 'Tis the hand of God
'Tis the hand of God that is writing on the wall; 'Tis the hand of God

The Handwriting on the Wall—Concluded.

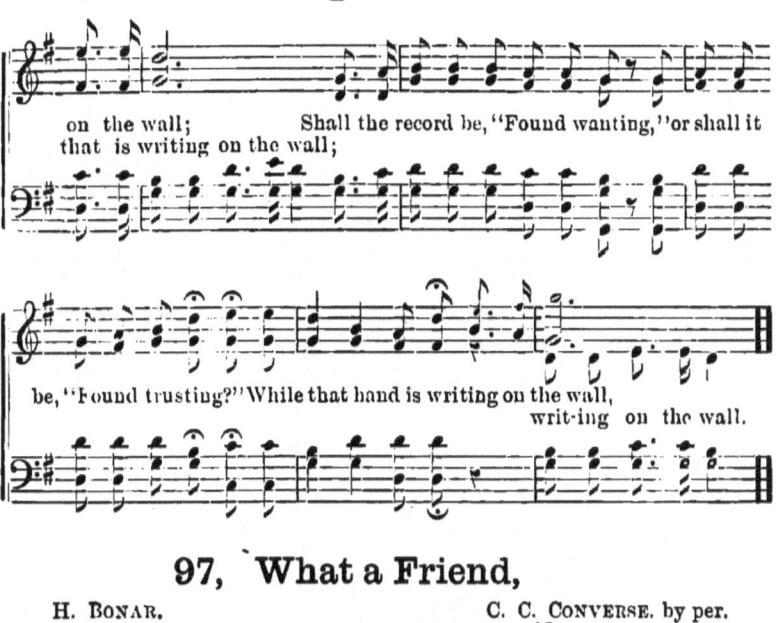

97, What a Friend,

H. BONAR.   C. C. CONVERSE. by per.

1. What a friend we have in Jesus, All our sins and griefs to bear! What a privilege to carry Ev-'ry thing to God in prayer! Oh, what peace we often forfeit, Oh, what needless pain we bear, All because we do not carry Ev-'ry thing to God in prayer!

2 Have we trials and temptations?
　Is there trouble anywhere?
We should never be discouraged,
　Take it to the Lord in prayer.
Can we find a friend so faithful,
　Who will all our sorrows share?
Jesus knows our every weakness,
　Take it to the Lord in prayer.

3 Are we weak and heavy-laden,
　Cumbered with a load of care?
Precious Savior, still our refuge,—
　Take it to the Lord in prayer.
Do thy friends despise, forsake thee?
　Take it to the Lord in prayer;
In His arms He'll take and shield thee
　Thou wilt find a solace there.

99. I'm going Home.

Rev. WILLIAM HUNTER. Arr. by WILLIAM MILLER, M. D.

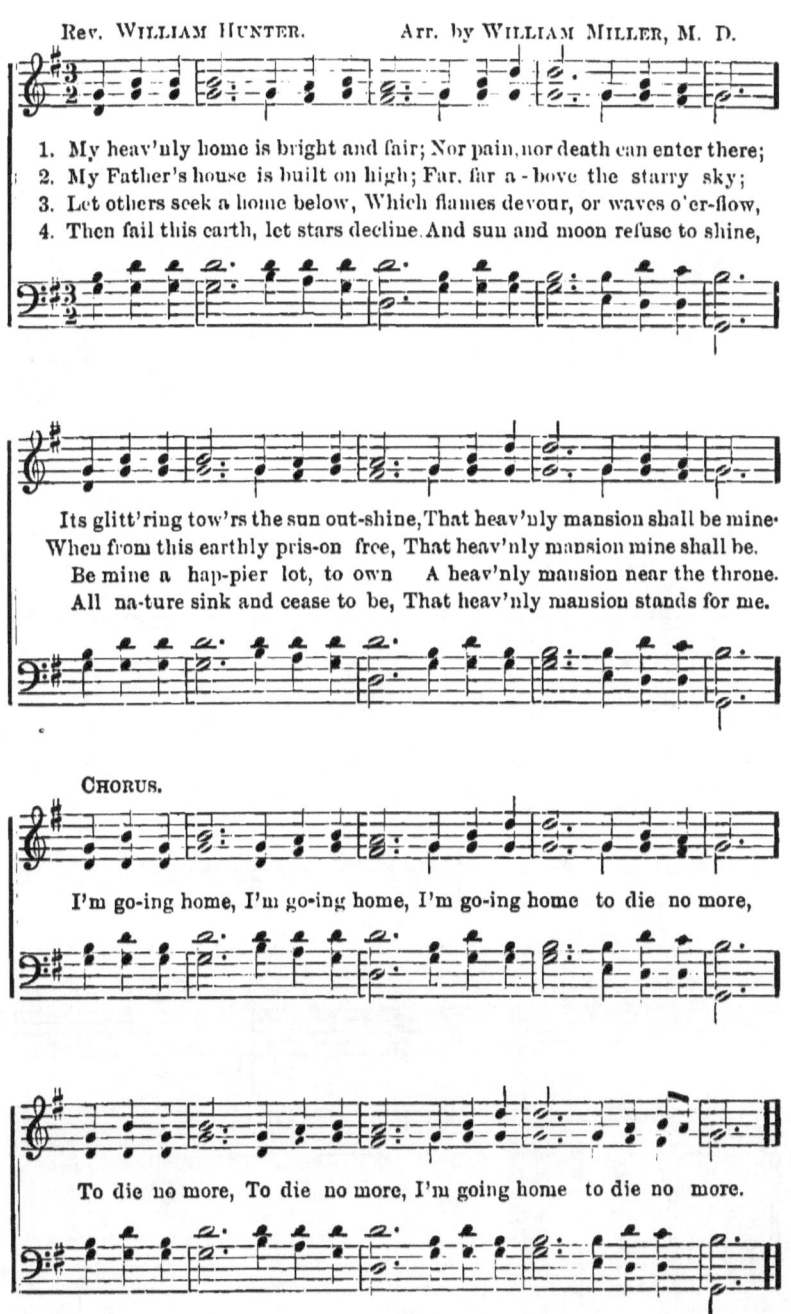

1. My heav'nly home is bright and fair; Nor pain, nor death can enter there;
2. My Father's house is built on high; Far, far a-bove the starry sky;
3. Let others seek a home below, Which flames devour, or waves o'er-flow,
4. Then fail this earth, let stars decline, And sun and moon refuse to shine,

Its glitt'ring tow'rs the sun out-shine, That heav'nly mansion shall be mine·
When from this earthly pris-on free, That heav'nly mansion mine shall be.
Be mine a hap-pier lot, to own A heav'nly mansion near the throne.
All na-ture sink and cease to be, That heav'nly mansion stands for me.

CHORUS.

I'm go-ing home, I'm go-ing home, I'm go-ing home to die no more,

To die no more, To die no more, I'm going home to die no more.

101. BE NOT DISCOURAGED.

J. V. COOMBS. J. T. REESE.

1. On-ward, broth-er, nev-er be dis-cour-aged, Christ is Cap-tain of the might-y throng; Je-sus bids you ev-er to be faith-ful, For-ward, stead-y, pass the word a-long.
2. Foes may rise, but let us nev-er fal-ter, Brave-ly bat-tle ev'-ry bar-rier down; Un-to those found ev-er true and val-iant, God will give an ev-er-last-ing crown.
3. Press on up-ward, shout a-loud ho-san-na, Christ is com-ing back to claim his own; He will give us home a-mong the an-gels, If we stand un-til the vict'ry's won.

CHORUS.
Cour-age, broth-er, come and join our ar-my, Faith and Hope will gain the vic-to-ry;

D.S.—Work on, pray on, keep the ban-ner float-ing, Till the gos-pel sets the peo-ple free.

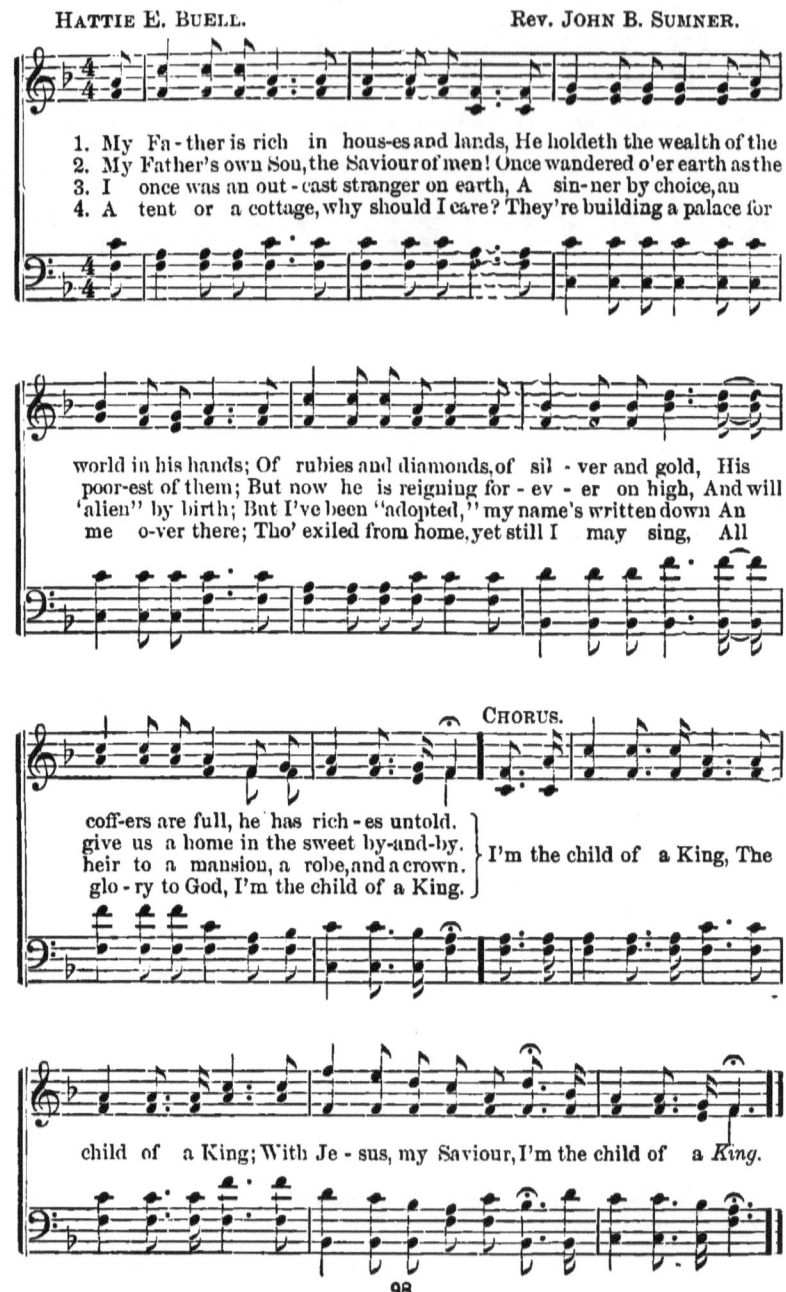

107. ON WHAT ARE YOU BUILDING, MY BROTHER?

H. R. TRICKETT. J. H. ROSECRANS.

1. On what are you build-ing, my broth-er? Your hopes of an e-ter-nal home, Is it loose, shifting sand, or the firm, sol-id rock, You are trust-ing for a-ges to come.
2. On one or the oth-er, my broth-er? You are building your hopes day by day; You are risk-ing your soul on the works that you do: Will the dark wa-ters sweep you a-way.
3. Your Sav-iour has warned you, my broth-er: I pray you, give heed to his voice; There is life on the rock, but there's death on the sand, Oh, my broth-er, pray tell me your choice.
4. No mat-ter how care-ful, my broth-er, The sand for your house you pre-pare, 'Twill be all swept away when the floods shall descend, Leav-ing noth-ing but death and des-pair.

CHORUS.

Hearing and doing, we build on the Rock, Hearing a-lone, we build on the sand; Both will be tried by the storm and the flood, On-ly the Rock the tri-al will stand.

112. SEND THE LIGHT.

C. H. G.   "Go into all the world."   CHAS. H. GABRIEL.

1. There's a call comes ringing o'er the restless wave, "Send the light! Send the
2. We have heard the Ma-ce-donian call to-day, "Send the light! Send the
3. Let us pray that grace may ev'rywhere abound, "Send the light! Send the
4. Let us not grow weary in the work of love, "Send the light! Send the

light!" There are souls to rescue, there are souls to save, Send the
light!" And a gold-en off-ring at the cross we lay, Send the
light!" And a Christ-like spir-it ev'-rywhere be found, Send the
light!" Let us gath-er jew-els for a crown a-bove, Send the

light! Send the light! Send the light, the bless-ed
Send the light, Send the light, Send the light, the

gos-pel light, Let it shine from shore to shore! Send the
blessed gospel light, let it shine, from shore to shore!

light! and let its radiant beams light the world for ever-more..........
Send the light! and let its radiant beams light the world for evermore.

By permission of CHAS. H. GABRIEL, owner of copyright.

113. OH, COULD I SPEAK.

S. MEDLEY.   DR. LOWELL MASON.

1. Oh, could I speak the match-less worth, Oh, could I sound the glories forth Which in my Sa-viour shine, I'd soar and touch the heav'nly strings, And vie with Ga-briel while he sings, In notes al-most di-vine, In notes al-most di-vine.
2. I'd sing the pre-cious blood he spilt, My ran-som from the dreadful guilt, Of sin and wrath di-vine! I'd sing his glo-rious righteousness, In which all per-fect heav'nly dress My soul shall ev-er shine, My soul shall ev-er shine.
3. Well—the de-light-ful day will come, When my dear Lord will bring me home, And I shall see his face: Then with my Sa-viour, Brother, Friend, A blest e-ter-ni-ty I'll spend, Tri-um-phant in his grace, Tri-um-phant in his grace.

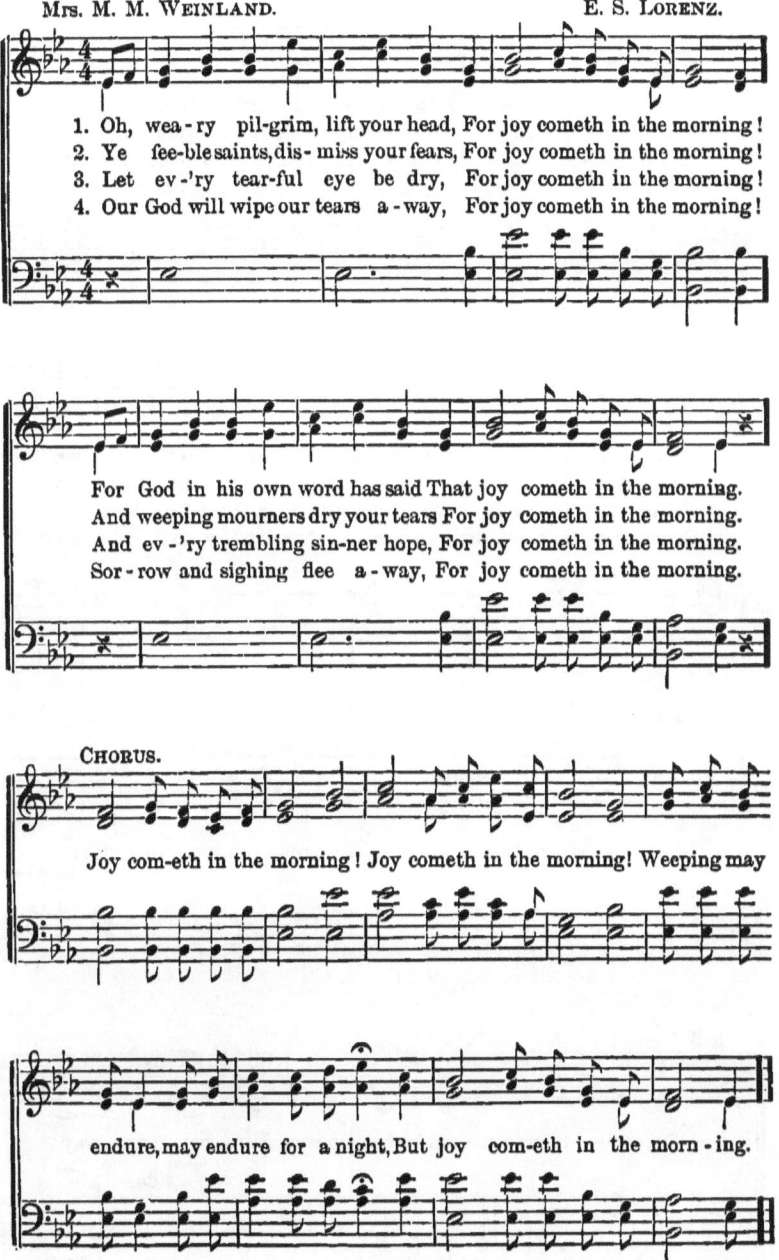

THE LORD IS THY REWARDER.—Concluded.

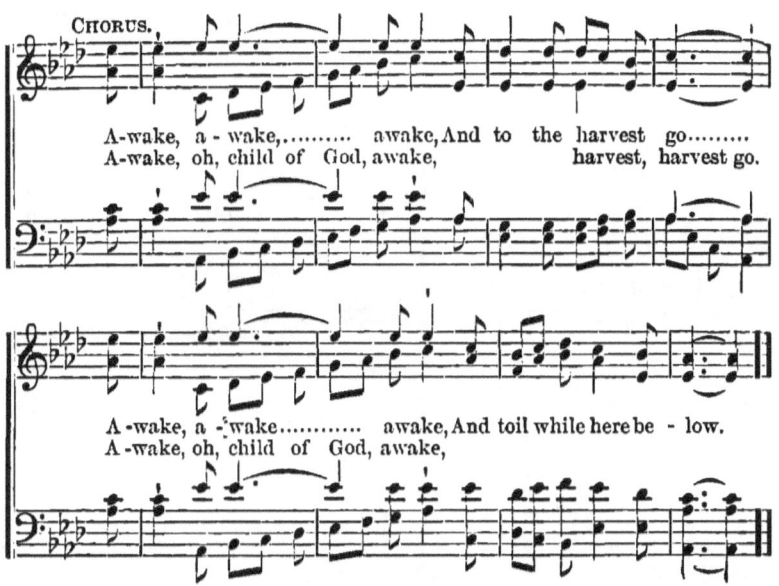

119. JESUS, SAVIOUR, PILOT ME.

J. E. GOULD.

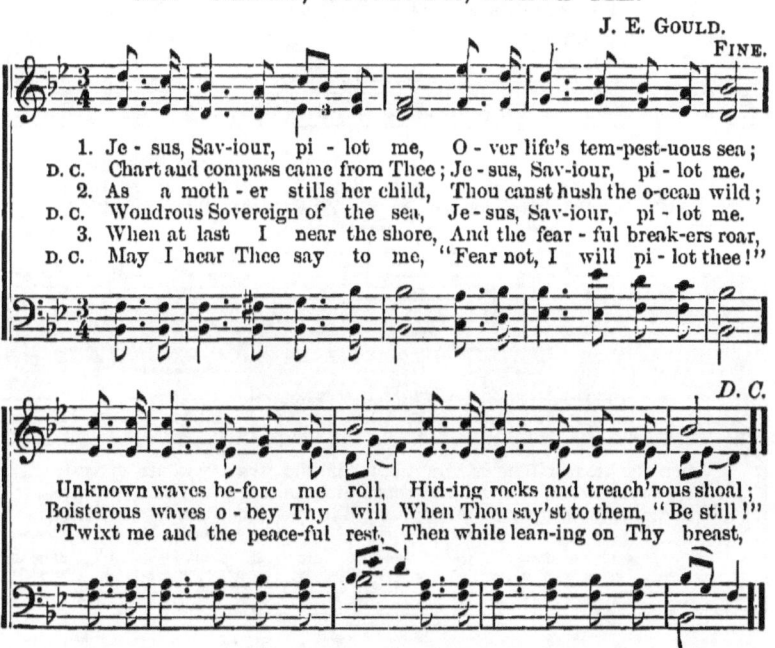

120. HAPPY ON THE WAY.

R. E. HUDSON.

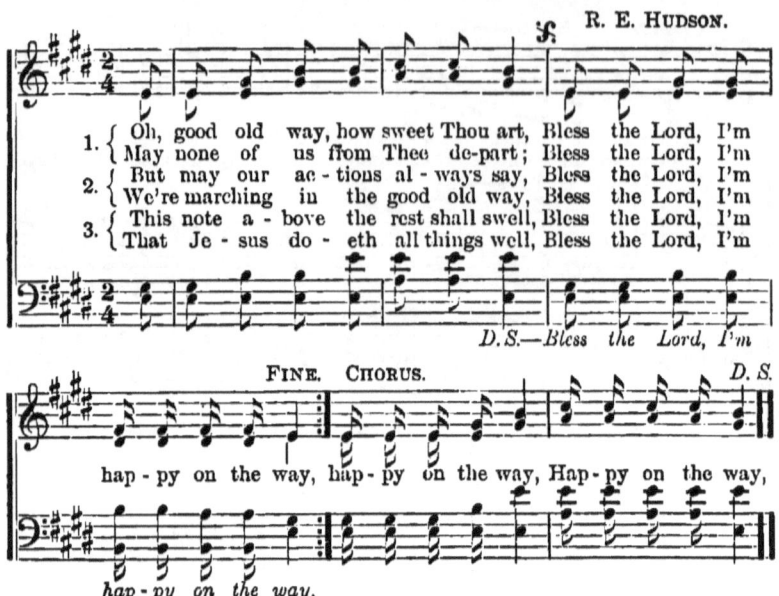

1. Oh, good old way, how sweet Thou art, Bless the Lord, I'm
   May none of us from Thee de-part; Bless the Lord, I'm
2. But may our ac-tions al-ways say, Bless the Lord, I'm
   We're marching in the good old way, Bless the Lord, I'm
3. This note a-bove the rest shall swell, Bless the Lord, I'm
   That Je-sus do-eth all things well, Bless the Lord, I'm

D.S.—Bless the Lord, I'm

FINE. CHORUS.   D. S.

hap-py on the way, hap-py on the way, Hap-py on the way,

hap-py on the way.

121. IS THERE ANY ROOM UP YONDER?

Rev. A. M. HOOTMAN.   W. E. M. HACKLEMAN.

SOLO OR DUET.

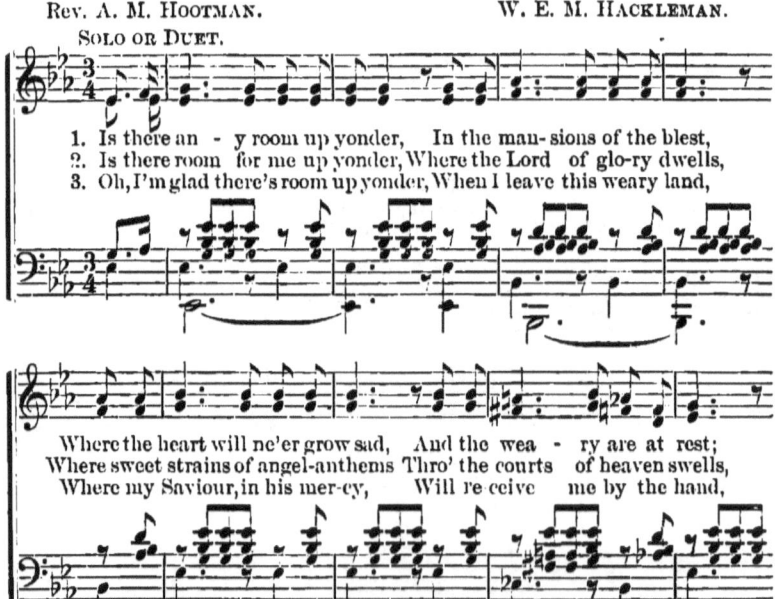

1. Is there an - y room up yonder, In the man-sions of the blest,
2. Is there room for me up yonder, Where the Lord of glo-ry dwells,
3. Oh, I'm glad there's room up yonder, When I leave this weary land,

Where the heart will ne'er grow sad, And the wea - ry are at rest;
Where sweet strains of angel-anthems Thro' the courts of heaven swells,
Where my Saviour, in his mer-cy, Will re-ceive me by the hand,

IS THERE ANY ROOM UP YONDER? Concluded.

In the shin-ing courts of glo-ry, Where our an-gel lov'd ones dwell,
In the home of bliss e-ter-nal, Where all hearts are fill'd with joy,
I was lost, a ru-ined sin-ner, But he came and died for me,

Is there an-y room for sin-ners? Tell me yes, and all is well?
Where death is but a stranger, And his pangs can-not an-noy?
And my sins are all for-giv-en, And my Sa-viour I shall see?

RESPONSIVE CHORUS.

Yes, my brother, in that ci-ty, In the land of E-ter-nal Day,
There is always room for sin-ners, Who be-lieve, repent, o-bey.

SWEET GOSPEL BELLS.—Concluded.

I WANT TO BE A WORKER.—Concluded.

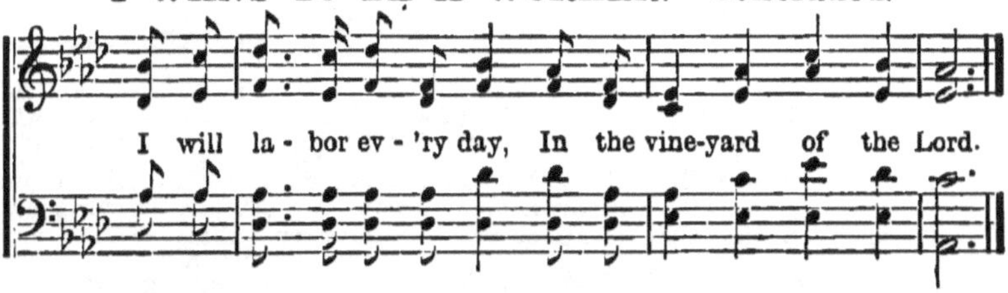

I will la-bor ev-'ry day, In the vine-yard of the Lord.

126. LORD'S DAY.

JOHN NEWTON.   DR. LOWELL MASON.

1. Safe-ly thro' an-oth-er week God has brought us on our way;
2. While we seek sup-plies of grace, Thro' the blest Re-deem-er's name,
3. Here we come Thy name to praise; Let us feel Thy presence near;

Let us each a bless-ing seek, Wait-ing in His courts to-day—
Show Thy rec-on-cil-ing face, Take a-way our sin and shame;
May Thy glo-ry meet our eyes, While we in Thy house ap-pear;

Day of all the week the best, Em-blem of e-ter-nal rest,
From our world-ly care set free, May we rest his day in Thee,
Here af-ford us, Lord, a taste Of our ev-er-last-ing rest,

Day of all the week the best, Emblem of e-ter-nal rest.
From our world-ly care set free, May we rest this day in Thee.
Here af-ford us, Lord, a taste, Of our ev-er-last-ing rest.

129. WHY DO YOU WAIT?

G. F. R.   Geo. F. Root, by per.

1. Why do you wait, dear broth-er, Oh, why do you tar-ry so long?
2. What do you hope, dear broth-er, To gain by a fur-ther de-lay?
3. Do you not feel, dear broth-er, His spir-it now striving with-in?
4. Why do you wait, dear broth-er, The harvest is pass-ing a-way,

Your Saviour is waiting to give you A place in His sanctified throng.
There's no one to save you but Je-sus, There's no oth-er way but His way.
Oh, why not accept His sal-va-tion, And throw off thy burden of sin?
Your Saviour is longing to bless you, There's danger and death in delay?

Chorus.

Why not? why not? Why not come to Him now? now?

130. I Hear the Saviour Say.

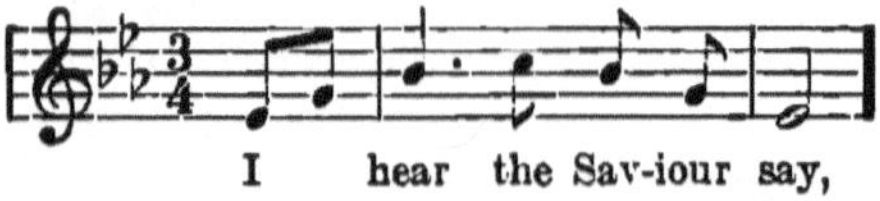

I hear the Sav-iour say,

1. I hear the Saviour say,
   Thy strength indeed is small;
   Child of weakness, watch and pray,
   Find in Me thine all in all.

Cho.—Jesus paid it all,
   All to Him I owe;
   Sin had left a crimson stain:
   He washed it white as snow.

2. Lord, now indeed I find
   Thy pow'r, and that alone,
   Can change the leper's spots,
   And melt the heart of stone.

3. For nothing good have I
   Where by Thy grace to claim—
   I'll wash my garments white
   In the blood of Calvary's Lamb

4. And when before the throne
   I stand in Him complete,
   I'll lay my trophies down,
   All down at Jesus' feet.

131. PRODIGAL CHILD.*

MRS. ELLEN H. GATES.   W. H. DOANE.

1. Come home! come home! You are wea-ry at heart,
2. Come home! come home! For we watch and we wait,
3. Come home! come home! From the sor-row and blame,
4. Come home! come home! There is bread and to spare,

For the way has been dark, And so lone-ly and wild;
And we stand at the gate, While the shad-ows are piled;
From the sin and the shame, And the tempt-er that smiled,
And a warm wel-come there; Then, to friends rec-on-ciled,

O, prod-i-gal child! Come home! oh come home!

CHORUS.
Come home, come home, Come, oh come home.
Come home, come home, come home.

* May be used as a Duet by using small notes with bass in octaves.

132. I Hear Thy Welcome Voice.

I hear Thy welcome voice,

1. I hear Thy welcome voice,
That calls me, Lord, to Thee!
For cleansing in Thy precious blood,
That flowed on Calvary.

Cho. I am coming, Lord,
Coming now to Thee!
Wash me, cleanse me in the blood,
That flowed on Calvary.

2. Though coming weak and vile,
Thou dost my strength assure;
Thou dost my vileness fully cleanse,
Till spotless all and pure.

3. 'Tis Jesus calls me on
To perfect faith and love,
To perfect hope and peace and trust,
For earth and heaven above.

4. And He assurance gives
To loyal hearts and true,
That every promise is fulfilled
To those who hear and do.

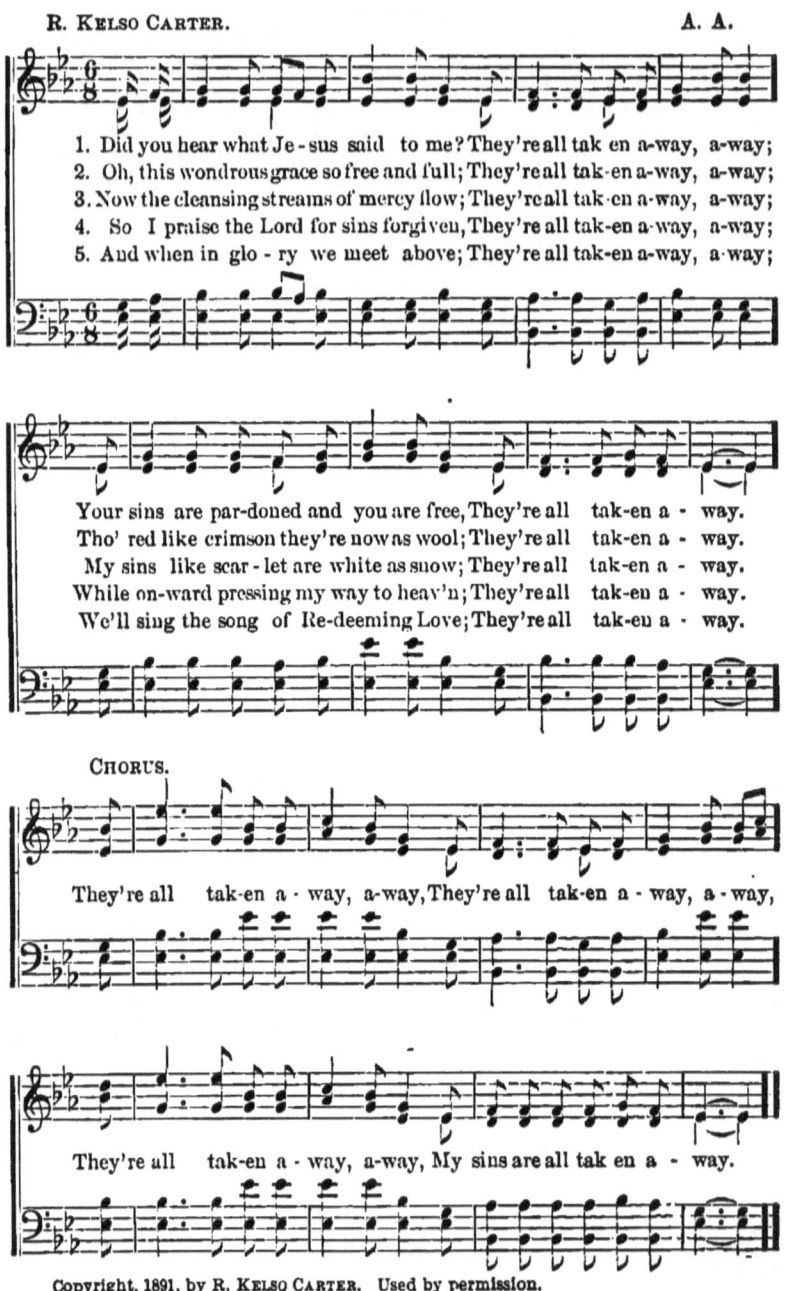

WHAT WILL YOU DO WITH JESUS? Concluded.

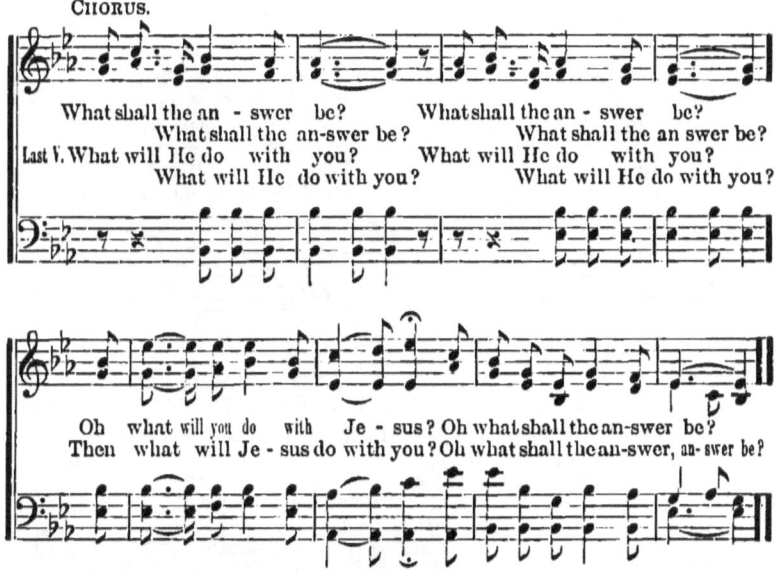

140. PRINCE OF PEACE.

MARY BARBER   Arr. from L. M. GOTTSCHALK.

1. Prince of peace, con-trol my will; Bid this struggling heart be still;
2. Thou hast bought me with Thy blood, O-pened wide the gate of God:
3. May Thy will, not mine, be done; May Thy will and mine be one;
4. Sav-iour, at Thy feet I fall; Thou, my Life, my God, my All.

Bid my fears and doubtings cease; Hush my Spir-it in-to peace.
Peace I ask—but peace must be, Lord, in be-ing one with Thee.
Chase these doubtings from my heart—Now Thy per-fect peace im-part.
Let Thy hap-py ser-vant be, One for-ev-er-more with Thee.

3. If you meet a soul discouraged,
   Going thro' the land,
   Show to him God's word of promise,
   Cheer him all you can.
   For deeds and words in kindness given,
   Mend the broken strand :
   A little help when one is drowning
   Often saves the man.

4. Would you have a home up yonder,
   In the better land?
   Do to others as you'd have them,
   Do to you my man.
   And when the Master comes for jewels,
   Searching thro' the land,
   He'll take thy weary faithful spirit
   Home to Beulah Land.

Copyrighted, 1895, W. E. M. Hackleman.

146. THE SINNER'S FEAR, AND CHRISTIAN'S HOPE.

Rev. A. W. Conner.   W. E. M. Hackleman.

1. Christians, I have heard you speak-ing, Of a ci-ty fair and bright, Where a joy-ous hap-py peo-ple, Clad in garments, pure and white, Freed from all earth's cares and sor-rows, Live thro' all e-ter-ni-ty; Tell me an-y place for me.
2. While my sins like fet-ters bind me, To this life of guilt and woe, There's no hope that I shall ev-er, A-ny joys in heav-en know, Oh dear Christ-ians I'm made wretched, Christ-ians, In that ci-ty, As the words to me you tell; I'm un-pure and righteous dwell.
3. Yes, I'll hope in Christ my Sav-iour, In His love I'll live each day, When temptations gath-er round me, I will choose "that living Way," Ho-ly Sav-iour! bless'd Re-deem-er! fit-ted for that ci-ty, Where the pare Thy need-y ser-vant, I ac-cept Thy won-drous love; Oh pre-ci-ty bright a-bove. For that

Copyright, 1895, by W. M. E. Hackleman.

The Sinner's Fear and Christian's Hope.—Continued.

*Repeat each sentence.

1. Yes, my bro - - ther in that ci - ty,
   Yes, my brother in that ci - ty, Yes, my bro-ther In that ci - ty
* 2. Je - sus Christ our eld - er bro-ther,
3. You can en - - ter now His kingdom,

There's a place, prepared for thee; For the
There's a place prepared for thee, There's a place prepared for thee; For the
Paid the debt............ we could not pay, By His
By con - fess - - ing His dear name, Thus con-

King, when He as - cend - ed, Left these
King when He as-cend - ed, For the King when He as-cen-ded, Left these
death, up - on the cross-tree, O - pened
fess - - ing and o - bey-ing, You can

words............ for you and me............
words for you and me, Left these words For you and me.
up............ a liv - ing way............
full - - - est par - don claim............

The Sinner's Fear and Christian's Hope.—Concluded.

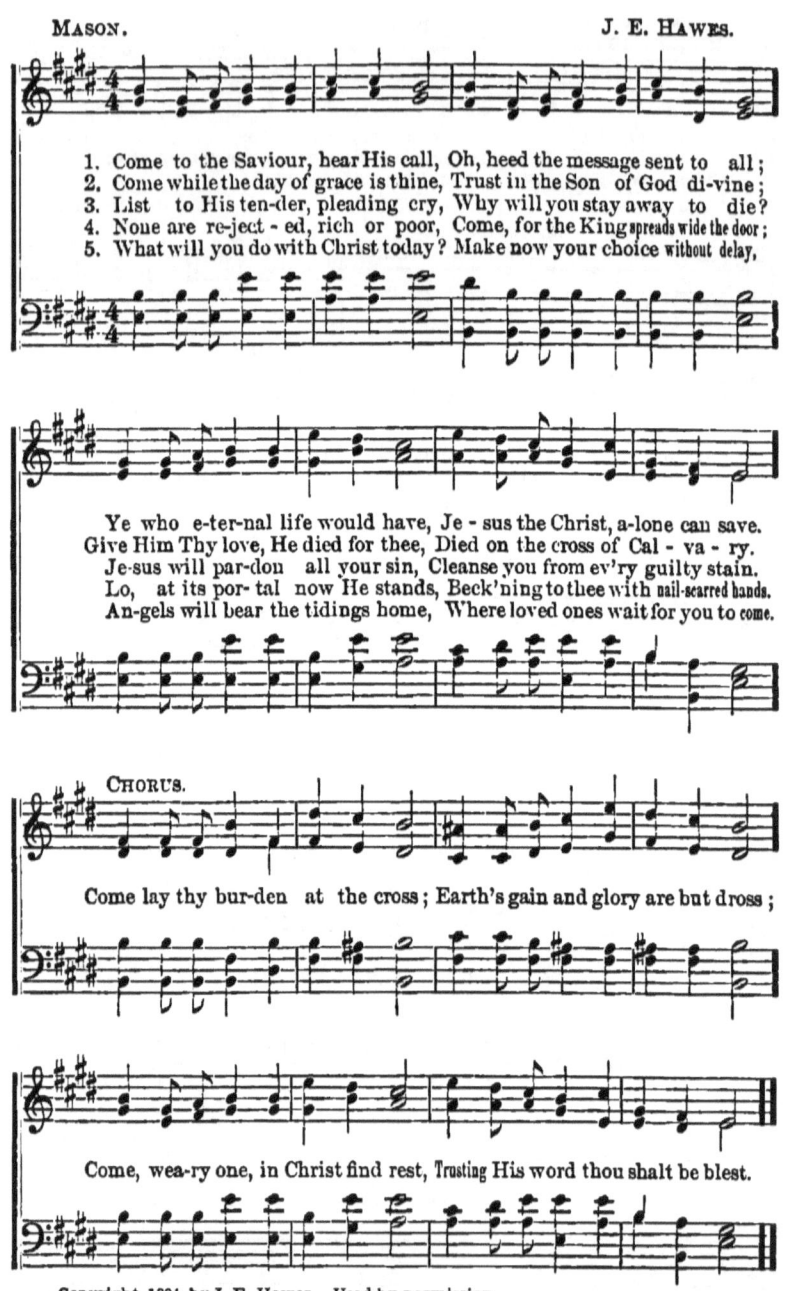

148. MORE ABOUT JESUS.

E. E. HEWITT.   JNO. R. SWENEY.

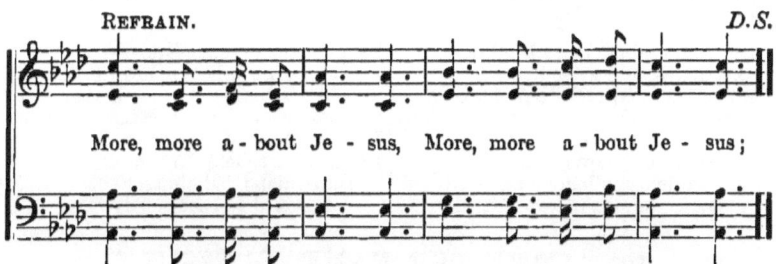

1. More a-bout Je-sus would I know, More of His grace to oth-ers show;
2. More a-bout Je-sus let me learn, More of His ho - ly will dis-cern;
3. More a-bout Je-sus; in His word, Holding communion with my Lord;
4. More a-bout Je-sus; on His throne, Rich-es in glo-ry all His own;

More of His sav - ing full-ness see, More of His love Who died for me.
Spir - it of God, my teach-er be, Showing the things of Christ to me.
Hear-ing His voice in ev - 'ry line, Making each faithful say - ing mine.
More of His kingdom's sure increase, More of His com-ing, Prince of Peace.

D. S.—More of His sav - ing full-ness see, More of His love who died for me.

REFRAIN.   *D. S.*

More, more a - bout Je - sus, More, more a - bout Je - sus;

149. I NEED THEE EVERY HOUR.

Key of A♭.

1. I need Thee every hour,
    Most gracious Lord,
    No tender voice like Thine
    Can peace afford.
CHO.—I need Thee, oh! I need Thee,
    Every hour I need Thee;
    O bless me now, my Saviour,
    I come to Thee.

2. I need Thee every hour,
    Stay Thou near by;
    Temptations lose their power
    When Thou art nigh.

3. I need Thee every hour:
    Teach me Thy will;
    And Thy rich promises
    In me fulfill.

150. HARK! TEN THOUSAND.

THOS. KELLEY.　　　　　　　　　　LOWELL MASON.

1. Hark! ten thousand harps and voi-ces Sound the note of praise a-bove!
Je-sus reigns, and heav'n re-joi-ces— Je-sus reigns, the God of love.
See, He sits on yonder throne: Je-sus rules the world alone.
Hal-le-lu-jah! hal-le-lu-jah! Je-sus rules the world a-lone.

2.
Jesus, hail! whose glory brightens
　All above, and gives it worth:
Lord of life, Thy smile enlightens,
　Cheers and charms Thy saints on earth;
When we think of love like thine,
Lord, we own it love divine.
　Hallelujah! hallelujah!
Lord, we own it love divine.

3.
King of glory, reign forever—
　Thine an everlasting crown:
Nothing from Thy love shall sever
　Those whom Thou hast made Thine own;
Happy objects of Thy grace,
Destined to behold Thy face.
　Hallelujah! hallelujah!
Destined to behold Thy face.

151. TAKE THE NAME OF JESUS.

LYDIA BAXTER.　　　　　　　　　　*Key of A.*

1. Take the name of Jesus with you,
　Child of sorrow and of woe:
It will joy and comfort give you;
　Take it, then, where'er you go.
CHO.—Precious name, O how sweet!
　Hope of earth and joy of heav'n;
Precious name, O how sweet!
　Hope of earth and joy of heav'n!

2. Take the name of Jesus ever,
　As a shield from every snare;

If temptations round you gather,
　Breathe that holy name in prayer.

3. O the precious name of Jesus,
　How it thrills our souls with joy,
When His loving arms receive us,
　And His songs our tongues employ.

4. At the name of Jesus bowing,
　Falling prostrate at His feet,
King of kings in heav'n we'll crown Him,
　When our journey is complete.

152. ANGEL BAND.

REV. JEFFERSON HASCALL, 1860. WM. B. BRADBURY, by per.

1. { My lat-est sun is sink-ing fast, My race is near-ly run;
   { My strongest tri-als now are past, My tri-umph is be-gun. }
2. { I know I'm nearing the ho-ly ranks Of friends and kin-dred dear,
   { For I brush the dews on Jordan's banks, The cross-ing must be near. }

CHORUS.
O come, angel band, come and around me stand, O, bear me away on your snowy wings, To my immortal home. O, bear me away on your snowy wings To my immortal home.

3. I've almost gained my heavenly home,
My spirit loudly sings;
Thy holy ones, behold, they come!
I hear the noise of wings.

4. O, bear my longing heart to Him
Who bled and died for me;
Whose blood now cleanses from all sin,
And gives me victory.

153. SWEET HOUR OF PRAYER.

W. W. WALFORD. *Key of D.*

1. Sweet hour of prayer, sweet hour of prayer,
That calls me from a world of care,
And bids me, at my Father's throne,
Make all my wants and wishes known!
In seasons of distress and grief
My soul has often found relief,
And oft escaped the tempter's snare,
By thy return, sweet hour of prayer.

2. Sweet hour of prayer, sweet hour of prayer,
Thy wings shall my petition bear
To Him whose truth and faithfulness
Engage the waiting soul to bless;
And since he bids me seek His face,
Believe His word, and trust His grace,
I'll cast on Him my every care,
And wait for thee, sweet hour of prayer.

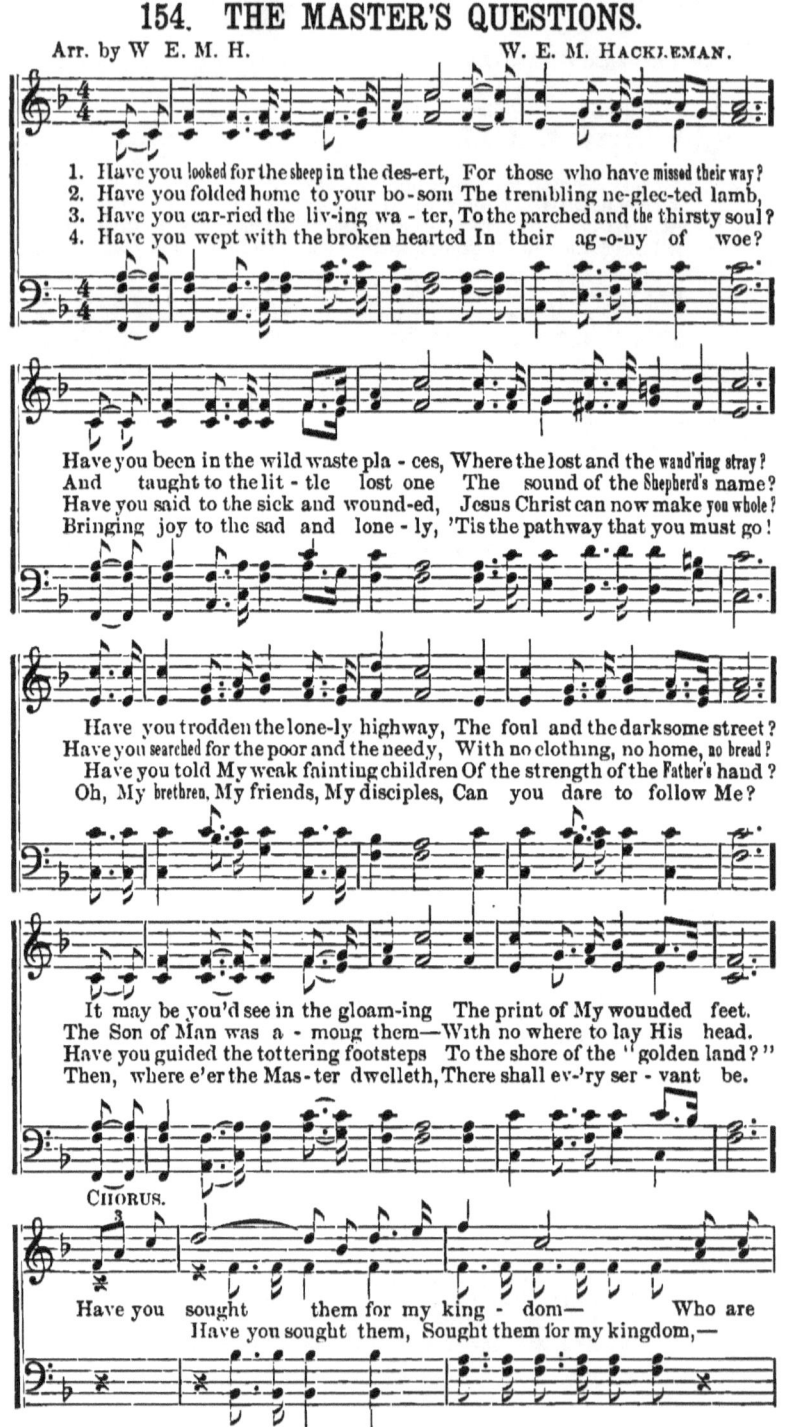

THE MASTER'S QUESTIONS. Concluded.

lost and wandering to-day, Have you told them of their
Who are lost and wandering to-day, Have you told them,
Sav - iour, And tried to help them on their way?
Told them of their Saviour, on their way?

155. COME, SOUND HIS PRAISE.

WATTS. ISAAC SMITH.

1. Come, sound His praise a-broad, And hymns of glo-ry sing;
Je-ho-vah is the sov-ereign God, The u-ni-ver-sal King.

2. Come, worship at His throne;
Come, bow before the Lord;
We are His work, and not our own;
He formed us by His word.

3. To-day attend His voice,
Nor dare provoke His rod;
Come, like the people of His choice,
And own your gracious God.

157. WONDERFUL WORDS OF LIFE.

"The words that I speak unto you, they are spirit, and they are life."—JOHN 6: 61.

P. P. BLISS.   P. P. BLISS, by per.

1. Sing them o-ver a-gain to me, Won-der-ful words of Life,
   Let me more of their beau-ty see, Won-der-ful words of (Omit.)
2. Christ, the blessed One gives to all Won-der-ful words of Life.
   Sin-ner, list to the lov-ing call, Won-der-ful words of (Omit.)
3. Sweet-ly ech-o the gos-pel call, Won-der-ful words of Life,
   Of-fer par-don and peace to all, Won-der-ful words of (Omit.)

Life, Words of life and beau-ty, Teach me faith and du-ty;
Life, All so free-ly giv-en, Woo-ing us to heav-en,
Life, Je-sus on-ly Sav-iour, Sanc-ti-fy for-ev-er,

Beautiful words, wonderful words, Wonderful words of Life, Life.

158. STAND UP FOR JESUS.

For Music, See No. 25.

1. Stand up, stand up for Jesus,
   Ye soldiers of the cross;
   Lift high His royal banner,
   It must not suffer loss;
   From victory unto victory
   His army shall He lead,
   Till every foe is vanquished
   And Christ is Lord indeed.

2. Stand up, stand up for Jesus,
   Stand in His strength alone;
   The arm of flesh will fail you;
   Ye dare not trust your own

Put on the gospel armor,
Each piece put on with prayer;
Where duty calls or danger,
Be never wanting there.

3. Stand up, stand up for Jesus,
   The strife will not be long;
   This day the noise of battle,
   The next the victor's song:
   To him that overcometh,
   A crown of life shall be;
   He with the King of glory
   Shall reign eternally.

159. REMEMBER ME.

RICHARD BURNHAM. ASA HULL.

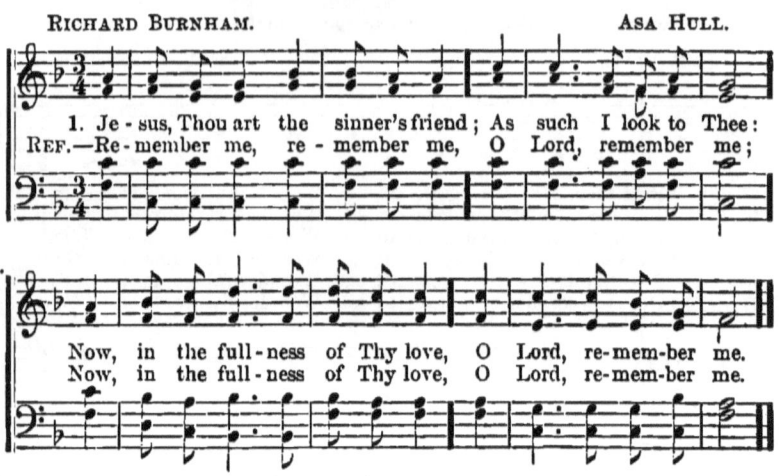

1. Jesus, Thou art the sinner's friend; As such I look to Thee:
Now, in the fullness of Thy love, O Lord, remember me.

REF.—Remember me, remember me, O Lord, remember me;
Now, in the fullness of Thy love, O Lord, remember me.

2. Remember Thy pure word of grace,
Remember Calvary;
Remember all Thy promises,
And then remember me.—REF.

3. Thou mighty Advocate with God,
I yield myself to Thee:
While Thou art sitting on Thy throne,
O Lord, remember me.—REF.

4. I own I'm guilty, own I'm vile;
Yet Thy salvation's free:
Then in Thy all-abounding grace,
O Lord, remember me.—REF.

5. And when I close my eyes in death,
And creature helps all flee,
Then, O my great Redeemer, Lord,
I pray, remember me.—REF.

160. LOVING HIM.

J. H. FILLMORE.

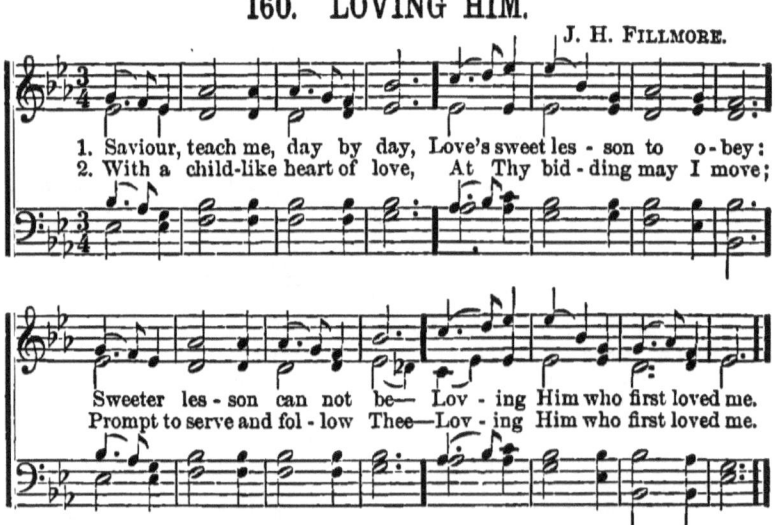

1. Saviour, teach me, day by day, Love's sweet lesson to obey:
Sweeter lesson can not be— Loving Him who first loved me.

2. With a child-like heart of love, At Thy bidding may I move;
Prompt to serve and follow Thee— Loving Him who first loved me.

3. Love in loving finds employ
In obedience all her joy;
Ever new that joy will be—
Loving Him who first loved me.

4. Teach me all Thy steps to trace,
Strong to follow in Thy grace;
Learning how to love from Thee—
Loving Him who first loved me.

161. HELP US, O LORD.

T. COTTERILL. HAYDN.

1. Help us, O Lord, Thy yoke to wear, De-light-ing in Thy will;
2. He that hath pi-ty on the poor, Doth lend un-to the Lord;

Each oth-ers bur-dens learn to bear; The law of love ful-fill.
And, lo! His rec-om-pense is sure, For more shall he re-stored.

3. To Thee our all devoted be,
   In Whom we move and live ;
   Freely we have received from Thee,
   And freely may we give.

4. And while we thus obey Thy word,
   And every want relieve,
   O may we find it, gracious Lord,
   More blest than to receive.

162. SUN OF MY SOUL.

J. KEBLE. Arr. by W. H. MONK.

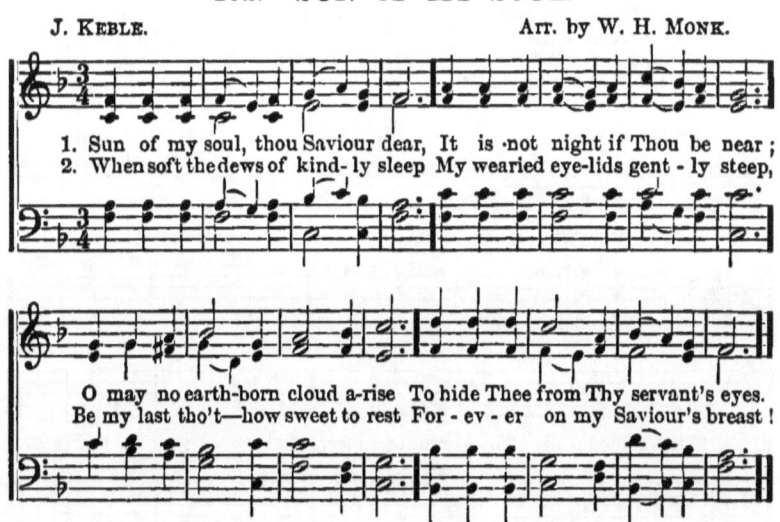

1. Sun of my soul, thou Saviour dear, It is not night if Thou be near;
2. When soft the dews of kind-ly sleep My wearied eye-lids gent-ly steep,

O may no earth-born cloud a-rise To hide Thee from Thy servant's eyes.
Be my last tho't—how sweet to rest For-ev-er on my Saviour's breast!

3. Abide with me from morn till eve,
   For without Thee I cannot live ;
   Abide with me when night is nigh,
   For without Thee I dare not die.

4. Be near to bless me when I wake,
   Ere thro' the world my way I take ;
   Abide with me till, in Thy love,
   I lose myself in heaven above.

163. HOW CAN I BUT LOVE HIM?

J. E. Rankin.   E. S. Lorenz.

1. So ten-der, so precious, My Sav-iour to me; So true and so gracious, I've found Him to be; How can I but love Him? But love Him, but love Him? There's no friend above Him, Poor sinner for thee.

2. So pa-tient, so kind-ly T'ward all of my ways; I blun-der so blindly— He love still re-pays;

3. Of all friends the fairest
And truest is He;
His love is the rarest
That ever can be—Ref.

4. His beauty, though bleeding
And circled with thorns,
Is then most exceeding,
For grief Him adorns.—Ref.

Anne Steele.

164. NAOMA.

H. G. Nageli.

1. Father; whate'er of earth-ly bliss Thy sovereign will de-nies, Ac-cepted at Thy throne of grace, Let this pe-ti-tion rise:

2. Give me a calm, a thankful heart,
From every murmur free;
The blessings of Thy grace impart,
And make me live to Thee;

3. Let the sweet hope that Thou art mine
My life and death attend;
Thy presence thro' my journey shine,
And crown my journey's end.

165. MY GRACIOUS REDEEMER.

B. FRANCIS.   GERMAN.

1. { My gracious Redeemer I love! His prais-es aloud I'll proclaim; }
   { And join with His armies a-bove, To shout His a-dor-a-ble name. }
D. C.—And feel them incessantly shine, My boundless in-ef-fa-ble joy.

2. { Earth's palaces, scepters, and crowns, Their pride with disdain I sur-vey; }
   { Their pomps are but shadows and sounds, And pass in a moment a-way. }
D. C.—My joy ev-er-last-ingly flows— My God, my Redeemer, is mine.

To gaze on His glories di-vine Shall be my e-ter-nal em-ploy.
The crown that my Saviour bestows Yon permanent sun shall outshine;

166. OLIVE'S BROW.

W. B. TAPPAN.   WM. B. BRADBURY.

1. 'Tis midnight, and on Ol-ive's brow The star is dimmed that lately shone;
2. 'Tis midnight; and from all remov'd, The Saviour wretles 'lone with fears;

'Tis midnight—in the garden now The suffering Saviour prays a-lone.
Ev'n that disciple whom He lov'd, Heeds not His Master's grief and tears.

3. 'Tis midnight, and for other's guilt
   The Man of Sorrows weeps in blood;
   Yet He that hath in anguish knelt
   Is not forsaken by His God.

4. 'Tis midnight, and from ether-plains
   Is borne the song that angels know,
   Unheard by mortals are the strains
   That sweetly soothe the Saviour's woe.

167. NIGHT WITH EBON PINION.

L. H. JAMESON. J. P. POWELL.

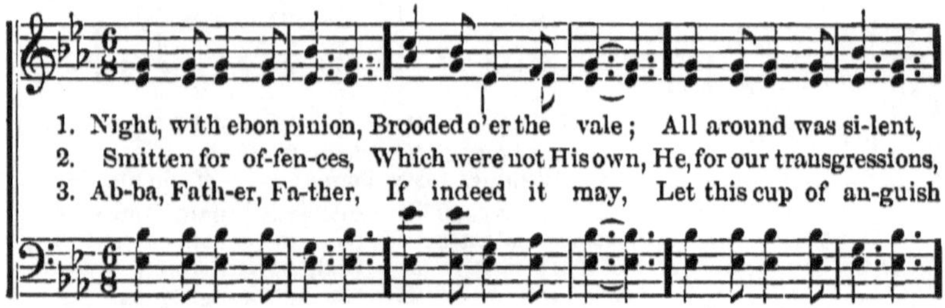

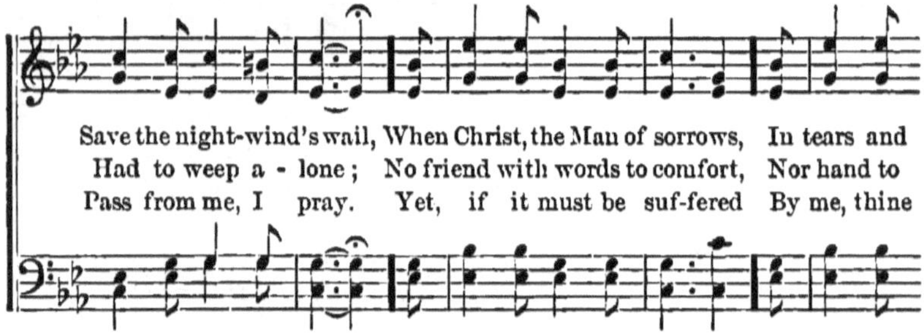

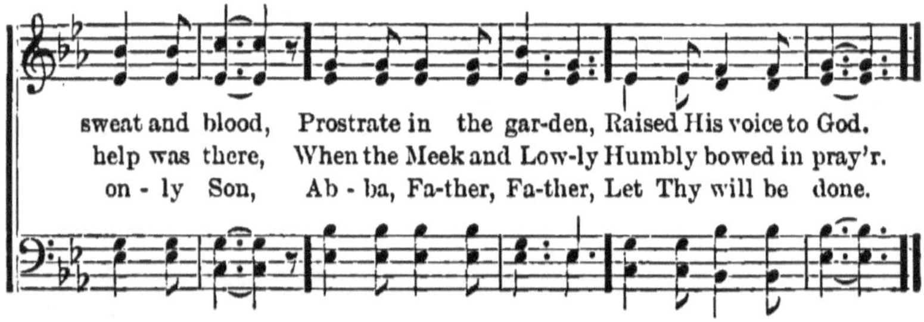

1. Night, with ebon pinion, Brooded o'er the vale; All around was si-lent, Save the night-wind's wail, When Christ, the Man of sorrows, In tears and sweat and blood, Prostrate in the gar-den, Raised His voice to God.
2. Smitten for of-fen-ces, Which were not His own, He, for our transgressions, Had to weep a-lone; No friend with words to comfort, Nor hand to help was there, When the Meek and Low-ly Humbly bowed in pray'r.
3. Ab-ba, Fath-er, Fa-ther, If indeed it may, Let this cup of an-guish Pass from me, I pray. Yet, if it must be suf-fered By me, thine on-ly Son, Ab-ba, Fa-ther, Fa-ther, Let Thy will be done.

168. SWEET DAY OF REST.

ISAAC WATTS. DANIEL READ.

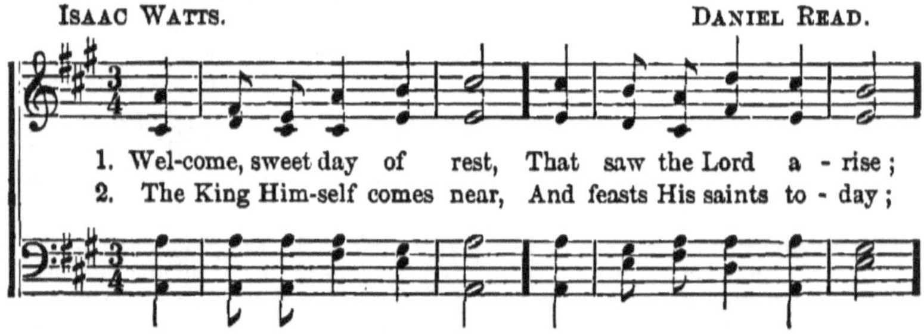

1. Wel-come, sweet day of rest, That saw the Lord a-rise;
2. The King Him-self comes near, And feasts His saints to-day;

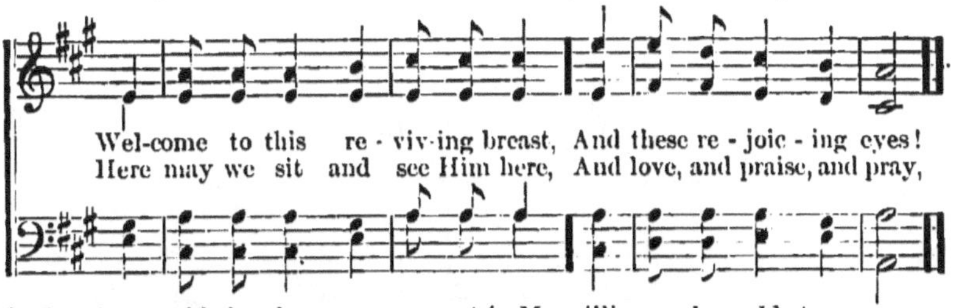

SWEET DAY OF REST, Concluded,

Wel-come to this re-viv-ing breast, And these re-joic-ing eyes!
Here may we sit and see Him here, And love, and praise, and pray,

3. One day, amid the place
Where my dear Lord hath been,
Is sweeter than ten thousand days
Within the tents of sin.

4. My willing soul would stay
In such a frame as this,
And sit and sing herself away
To everlasting bliss.

169. HE CAME TO SAVE ME.

H. E. BLAIR. WM. J. KIRKPATRICK.

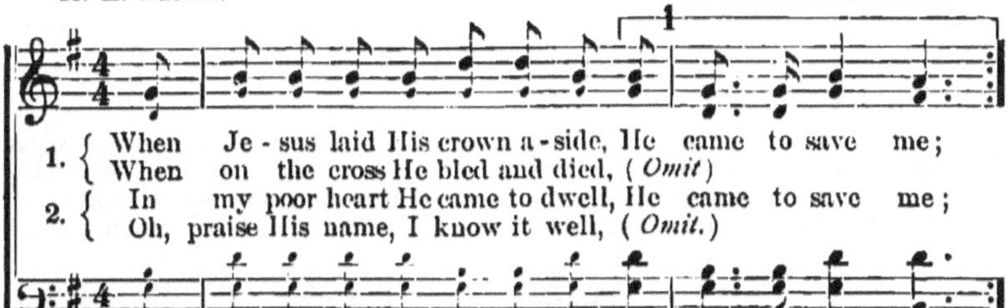

1. { When Je-sus laid His crown a-side, He came to save me;
    When on the cross He bled and died, (*Omit*) }
2. { In my poor heart He came to dwell, He came to save me;
    Oh, praise His name, I know it well, (*Omit*.) }

REFRAIN.
He came to save me. I'm so glad, I'm so glad,
I'm so glad that Je-sus came, And grace is free, (*Omit*)
He (*Omit*.) came to save me.

3. With gentle hand He leads me still,
He came to save me:
And trusting Him, I fear no ill,
He came to save me.

4. To Him my faith with rapture clings,
He came to save me.
To Him my heart looks up and sings,
He came to save me.

Copyright, 1885, by Wm. J. Kirkpatrick. Used by per.

170. EVENING BLESSING.

J. Edmeston. D. E. Jones.

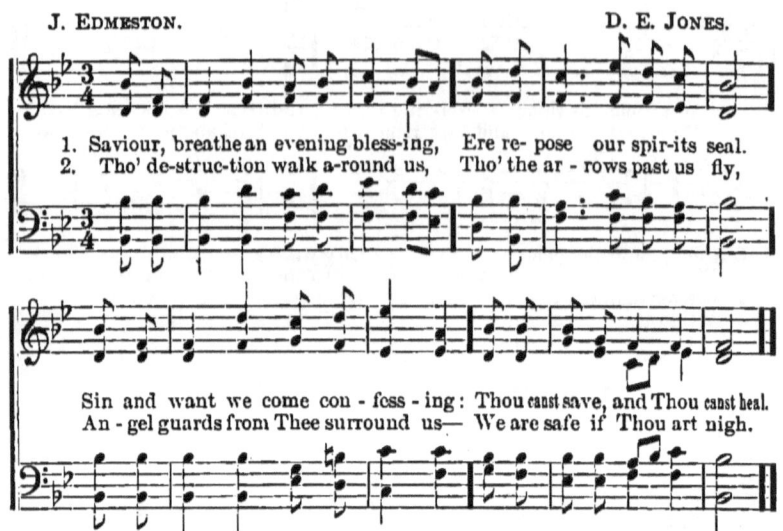

1. Saviour, breathe an evening bless-ing, Ere re- pose our spir-its seal.
   Sin and want we come con - fess - ing: Thou canst save, and Thou canst heal.
2. Tho' de-struc-tion walk a-round us, Tho' the ar - rows past us fly,
   An - gel guards from Thee surround us— We are safe if Thou art nigh.

3. Though the night be dark and dreary,
   Darkness can not hide from Thee;
   Thou art He who, never weary,
   Watchest where Thy people be.

4. Should swift death this night o'ertake us,
   And our couch become our tomb,
   May the morn in heaven awake us,
   Clad in bright and deathless bloom.

171. SONGS OF PRAISE.

J. Montgomery. Mozart.

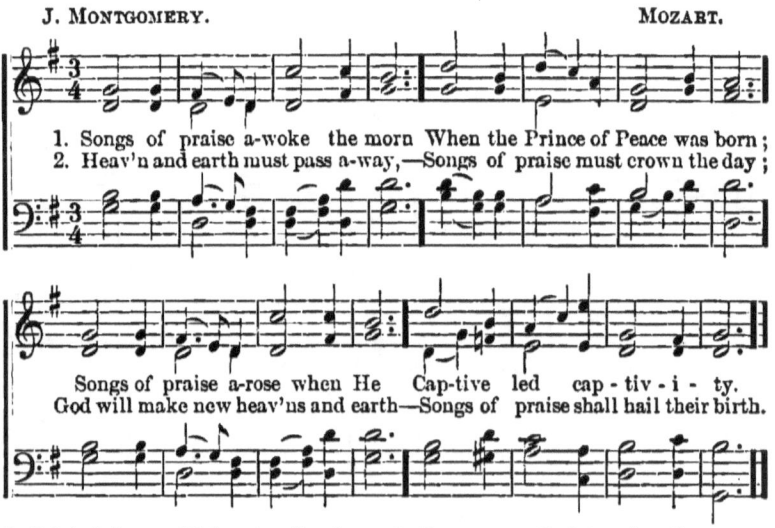

1. Songs of praise a-woke the morn When the Prince of Peace was born;
   Songs of praise a-rose when He Cap-tive led cap - tiv - i - ty.
2. Heav'n and earth must pass a-way,—Songs of praise must crown the day;
   God will make new heav'ns and earth—Songs of praise shall hail their birth.

3. Saints below, with heart and voice,
   Still in songs of praise rejoice,
   Learning here, by faith and love,
   Songs of praise to sing above.

4. Borne upon the latest breath,
   Songs of praise shall conquer death;
   Then, amidst eternal joy,
   Songs of praise their powers employ.

172. KING JESUS, REIGN,

RALF WARDLOW. L. O. EMERSON.

1. King Jesus, reign for- ev- er- more, Un-ri-valed in Thy courts above,
2. No oth-er Lord but Thee we'll know, No other pow'r but Thine confess;

While we, with all Thy saints, adore The wonders of re-deem-ing love.
We'll spread Thine honors while below, And heav'n shall hear us shout Thy grace.

3. We'll sing along the heavenly road
That leads us to Thy blest abode;
Till, with the vast, unnumbered throng,
We join in heaven's triumphant song:

4. Till, with pure hands and voices sweet,
We cast our crowns at Jesus' feet,
And sing of everlasting love,
In everlasting strains above.

173. WHEN I SURVEY,

ISAAC WATTS. Arr. by LOWELL MASON.

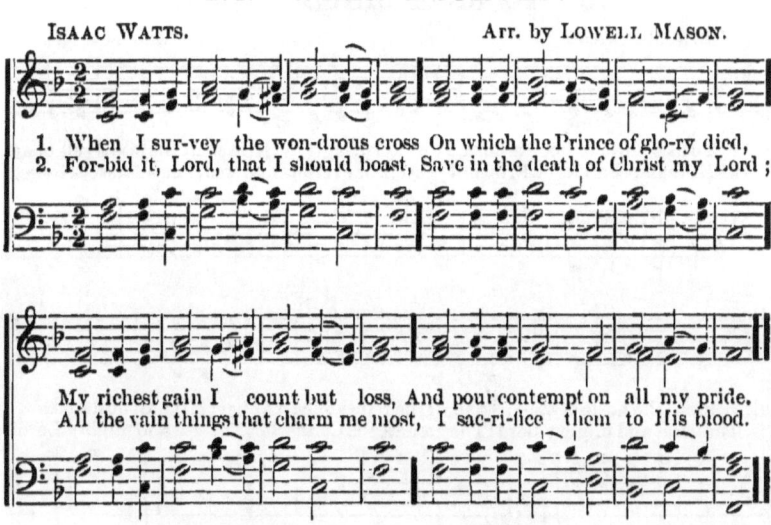

1. When I sur-vey the won-drous cross On which the Prince of glo-ry died,
2. For-bid it, Lord, that I should boast, Save in the death of Christ my Lord;

My richest gain I count but loss, And pour contempt on all my pride.
All the vain things that charm me most, I sac-ri-fice them to His blood.

3. See, from His head, His hands, His feet,
Sorrow and love flow mingled down;
Did e'er such love and sorrow meet,
Or thorns compose so rich a crown?

4. Were the whole realm of nature mine,
That were a present far too small;
Love so amazing, so divine,
Demands my soul, my life, my all.

174. AWAKE, MY TONGUE.

JOHN NEEDHAM.   JOHN HATTON.

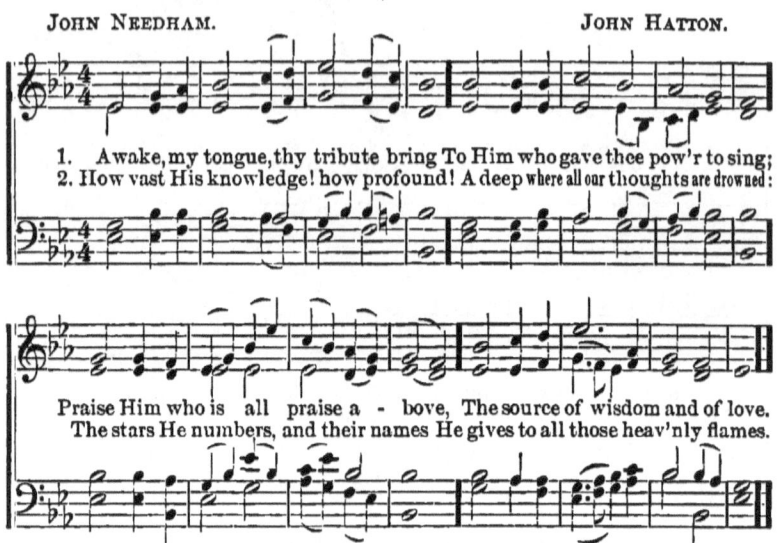

1. Awake, my tongue, thy tribute bring To Him who gave thee pow'r to sing;
2. How vast His knowledge! how profound! A deep where all our thoughts are drowned:

Praise Him who is all praise a - bove, The source of wisdom and of love.
The stars He numbers, and their names He gives to all those heav'nly flames.

3. Thro' each bright world above, behold
Ten thousand thousand charms unfold;
Earth, air, and mighty seas combine
To speak His wisdom all divine.

4. But in redemption, O what grace!
Its wonders, O what thought can trace!
Here wisdom shines forever bright;
Praise Him, my soul, with sweet delight.

175. TO US A CHILD IS BORN.

JOHN MORRISON   LOWELL MASON.

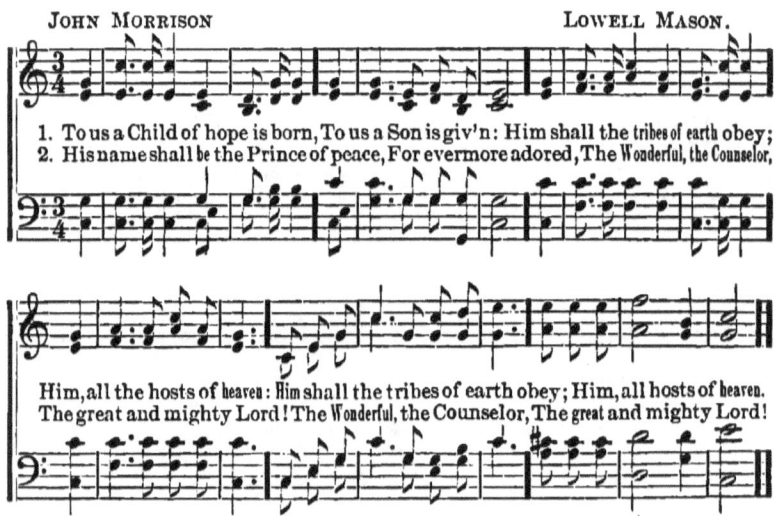

1. To us a Child of hope is born, To us a Son is giv'n: Him shall the tribes of earth obey;
2. His name shall be the Prince of peace, For evermore adored, The Wonderful, the Counselor,

Him, all the hosts of heaven: Him shall the tribes of earth obey; Him, all hosts of heaven.
The great and mighty Lord! The Wonderful, the Counselor, The great and mighty Lord!

3. His power, increasing, still shall spread;
His reign no end shall know;
Justice shall guard His throne above,
And peace abound below.

4. To us a Child of hope is born,
To us a Son is given;
The Wonderful, the Counselor,
The mighty Lord of heaven!

176. PRAISE THE SAVIOUR'S NAME.

J. V. C.   J. V. Coombs.

1. The Lord has saved me from my sins, Yes, He has made me free,
2. I put my trust in Christ the Lord, My voice to Him I'll raise,
3. Oh, sinner, come accept His name, Repent, obey His word,

And now He bids me follow Him, And He my friend will be.
I'll tell the story of His love. In songs of grateful praise.
Confess the Christ the Son of God, And He will be your Lord.

CHORUS.

Praise the Saviour's name, Praise His holy name, Oh, Jesus Christ God's only Son, Praise His holy name.

177. I GAVE MY LIFE FOR THEE.

Miss F. R. Havergal.   *Key of C.*

1. I gave my life to thee,
 My precious blood I shed,
That thou might'st ransomed be,
 And quickened from the dead.
I gave, I gave my life for thee:
What hast thou given for Me?

2. My Father's house of light,
 My glory-circled throne,
I left—for earthly night,
 For wanderings sad and lone.
I left, I left it all for thee:
Hast thou left aught for Me?

3. I suffered much for thee—
 More than thy tongue can tell,
Of bitterest agony,
 To rescue thee from hell.
I've borne, I've borne it all for thee:
What hast thou borne for Me?

4. And I have brought to thee,
 Down from my home above,
Salvation full and free,
 My pardon and my love.
I bring, I bring rich gifts to thee:
What hast thou brought to Me?

178. IN THE CROSS OF CHRIST.

J. BOWRING.   I. CONKEY.

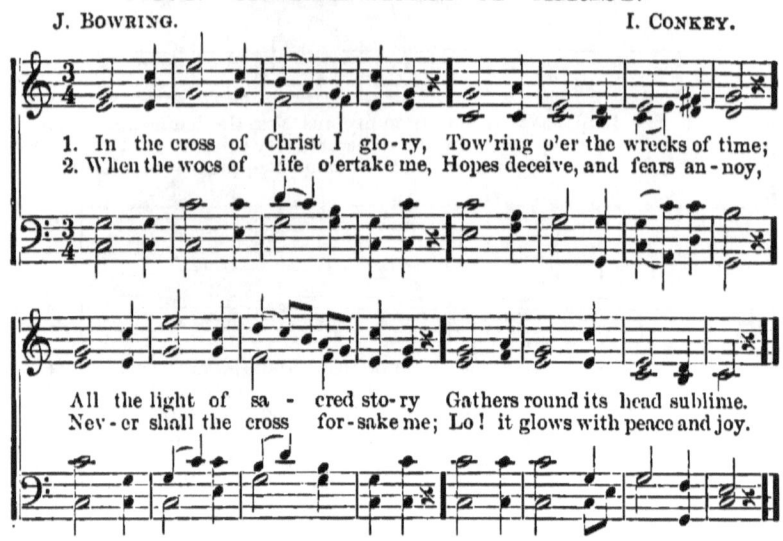

1. In the cross of Christ I glo-ry, Tow'ring o'er the wrecks of time;
2. When the woes of life o'ertake me, Hopes deceive, and fears an-noy,

All the light of sa-cred sto-ry Gathers round its head sublime.
Nev-er shall the cross for-sake me; Lo! it glows with peace and joy.

3. When the sun of bliss is beaming
Light and love upon my way,
From the cross the radiance, streaming,
Adds more lustre to the day.

4. Bane and blessing, pain and pleasure,
By the cross are sanctified,
Peace is there, that knows no measure,
Joys that through all time abide.

179. AWAKE AND SING.

WM. HAMMOND.   THOS. HASTINGS.

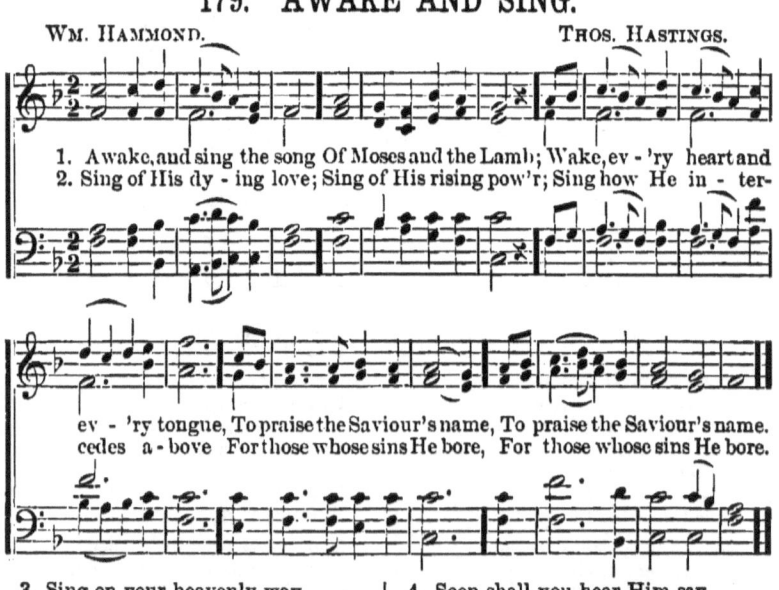

1. Awake, and sing the song Of Moses and the Lamb; Wake, ev-'ry heart and
2. Sing of His dy-ing love; Sing of His rising pow'r; Sing how He in-ter-

ev-'ry tongue, To praise the Saviour's name, To praise the Saviour's name.
cedes a-bove For those whose sins He bore, For those whose sins He bore.

3. Sing on your heavenly way,
You ransomed sinners, sing;
Sing on, rejoicing every day
In Christ, the glorious King.

4. Soon shall you hear Him say,
"You blessed children, come!"
Soon will He call you hence away,
And take His pilgrims home.

180. PRAISE THE LORD.

Praise the Lord; ye heav'ns, a-dore Him; Praise Him, angels in the height; Sun and moon, rejoice before Him; Praise Him, all ye stars of light, Hal-le-lujah! Amen, A-men, A-men, A-men.

2. Praise the Lord: for He hath spoken;
Worlds His mighty voice obeyed;
Laws which never shall be broken,
For their guidance He hath made.
3. Praise the Lord: for He is glorious;
Never shall His promise fail;
God hath made His saints victorious;
Sin and death shall not prevail.
4. Praise the God of our salvation;
Hosts on high His power proclaim;
Heaven and earth, and all creation,
Laud and magnify His name.

181. Near the Cross.
Key of G.

1. Jesus, keep me near the cross:
There a precious fountain,
Free to all, a living stream,
Flows from Calvary's mountain.

Chorus :—
In the cross, in the cross,
Be my glory ever,
Till my raptured soul shall find
Rest beyond the river.

2. Near the cross a trembling soul,
Love and mercy found me;
There the bright and morning star
Sheds its beams around me.
3. Near the cross! O Lamb of God,
Bring its scenes before me;
Help me walk from day to day,
With its shadows o'er me.
—F. C. VAN ALSTYNE.

182. Almost Persuaded.
Key of G.

1. "Almost persuaded" now to believe;
"Almost persuaded" Christ to receive.
Seems now some soul to say,
"Go, Spirit, go thy way,
Some more convenient day
On thee I'll call."

2. "Almost persuaded," come, come to-day;
"Almost persuaded," turn not away.
Jesus invites you here,
Angels are lingering near,
Prayers rise from hearts so dear:
O wanderer, come!

3. "Almost persuaded," harvest is past;
"Almost persuaded," doom comes at last;
"Almost" can not avail;
"Almost" is but to fail—
Sad, sad that bitter wail—
"Almost, but lost!"

WHERE'ER THOU GOEST. Concluded.

Just where, or how, I do not know, But thou'lt not lead a-stray.
A faithful guide Thou art I know, So close to Thee I'll keep.

D. S.—Where'er Thou goest I will go, Thro' all life's wea-ry way.

CHORUS.

Wher-e'er Thou go-est I will go, Near Thee I'll keep each day.

3. Where'er Thou goest I will go,
Though in some lonely dell;
Thou wilt be there—how sweet to know:
And cheerless hours dispel.

4. Where'er Thou goest I will go,
Through all my life's rough way;
And, at its end, I'll pass, I know,
Into an endless day.

185. NEARER, MY GOD, TO THEE.

MRS. S. F. ADAMS. LOWELL MASON.

1. Near-er, my God, to Thee, Near-er, to Thee; E'en tho' it be a cross
2. Tho' like the wan-der-er, Daylight all gone, Darkness be o-ver me,

D. S.—Near-er, my God, to Thee,

That rais-eth me! Still all my song shall be, Near-er, my God, to Thee!
My rest a stone; Yet, in my dreams I'd be Near-er, my God, to Thee,

Near-er to Thee.

3. There let the way appear,
Steps unto heaven;
All that Thou sendest me,
In mercy given;
Angels to beckon me
Nearer, my God, to Thee,
Nearer to Thee.

4. Or if, on joyful wing,
Cleaving the sky,
Sun, moon, and stars forgot,
Upward, I fly;
Still all my song shall be,
Nearer, my God, to Thee!
Nearer to Thee!

Wm. H. Keyser & Co. Phila., Pa.

INDEX.

A
	No.
All Hail the Power of Jesus' Name	56
Almost Persuaded	182
All Taken Away	137
Am I a Soldier of the Cross	39
Angel Band	152
Angels Hovering Round	94
Arouse Thee!	133
Asleep in Jesus	75
At the Cross	3
At the Door	59
Awake and Sing	179
Awake, My Tongue	174

B
Behold the Crucified One	117
Be Not Discouraged	101
Bid Him Come In	142
Blessed Assurance	69
Blessed be the Name	128
Bless Be the Tie	5
Bless the Lord	18
Bring Them In	106
Bringing in the Sheaves	24

C
Calling Me Over the Tide	37
Christ for the World and the World for Christ	108
Christ is Precious	85
Come	147
Come Home To-night	83
Come, Sinner, Come!	104
Come, Sound His Praises	155
Come to Jesus	11
Come to the Saviour	98
Come to the Saviour To-day	50
Come Unto Me	51
Communion	74
Consecration	63
Cross and Crown	35
Crown Him Lord of All	28

D
Decide To-night	105
Deliverance Will Come	80
Down in the Licensed Saloon	43
Doxology	77

E
Evening Blessing	170

F
Flee as Bird	95
Follow Me	2
For You and Me	48

G
	No.
Gathering Home	10
Going Home	99
God Be With You	14
Going Thro' the Land	145

H
Happy Children	33
Happy Day	23
Happy on the Way	120
Hark! Ten Thousand	150
Healing at the Fountain	7
He Came to Save Me	169
He Leadeth Me	183
Help Us, O Lord	161
Hosanna	46
How Can I But Love Him?	103

I
I Am Coming to the Cross	92
I Gave My Life for Thee	177
I Hear the Saviour Say	130
I Hear Thy Welcome Voice	132
I Know Not	42
I Long to be There	6
I Love Thy Kingdom	93
In the Cross of Christ	178
I Need Thee Every Hour	149
In the Shadow of the Rock	62
Is My Name Written There?	9
Is There Any Room Up Yonder?	121
I Want to be a Worker	125
I Will Follow Jesus	127

J
Jesus is Calling To-day	31
Jesus is Coming Again	89
Jesus, Lover of My Soul	41
Jesus Died for You	66
Jesus Saves	44
Jesus, Saviour, Pilot Me	119
Joy Cometh in the Morning	115
Joy to the World	57
Just as I Am	58

K
King Jesus Reigns	172

L
Lead Me Gently Home, Father	84
Lead Me Safely On	45
Leaning on the Everlasting Arms	124
Life's Story in Song	143
Lights Along the Shore	109
Leona,—Coming Back at Mem'ry's Call	123
Lo, I Am With You	71
Lord's Day	126
Loving Him	160

INDEX.

M
Title	No.
Memories of Galilee	61
More About Jesus	148
More Like Jesus	21
My Ain Countrie	81
My Country, 'Tis of Thee	91
My Gracious Redeemer	165
My Happy Home	29

N
Title	No.
Naoma	164
Nearer Home	30
Nearer, My God, to Thee	185
Near the Cross	181
Night With Ebon Pinion	167
No Sorrow There	88

O
Title	No.
Oh, Could I Speak	113
Oh, Sinner, Hear the Saviour's Call	116
Oh, When Shall I See Jesus?	25
Olivet	13
Olive's Brow	166
On What are You Building, My Brother?	107
Our Saviour	141
Over the River	34

P
Title	No.
Praise the Saviour's Name	176
Prince of Peace	140
Praise the Lord	180
Prodigal Child	131

R
Title	No.
Redeemed	138
Refuge	156
Remember Me	159
Revive Us Again	17
Rock of Ages	27

S
Title	No.
Sailing O'er the Sea	32
Saviour Wash Me in the Blood	20
Scatter Sunshine	19
Seeking the Lost	76
Send the Light	112
Shout the Tidings	53
Songs of Praise	171
Sound the Battle Cry	73
Standing on the Promises	144
Stand Up for Jesus	158
Sun of My Soul	162
Sunshine in My Soul	134
Sweet By-and-By	72
Sweet Day of Rest	168
Sweet Gospel Bells	122
Sweet Hour of Prayer	153

T
Title	No.
Take Me as I Am	49
Take the Name of Jesus With You	151
Tarry With Me	64
Tell it Again	82
Tell it to Jesus	8
Tell the Good News	110
Then Rejoice All Ye Ransomed	12
That's Enough for Me	1
The Angel's Welcome	60
The Best Friend is Jesus	4
The Child of a King	102
The Fountain of Life	36
The Great Physician	78
The Half Has Never Been Told	135
The Handwriting on the Wall	96
The Home for Me	22
The Home Over There	90
The Lord is Thy Rewarder	118
The Master's Questions	154
The Model Church	87
The Open Gate	40
The Rock That is Higher Than I	100
The Saviour's Call	103
The Sinner and the Song	79
The Sinner's Fear and Christian's Hope	146
There is a Fountain	65
There is a Great Day Coming	16
They Sing a New Song	47
Toiling for Jesus	15
Too Late	111
To Us a Child is Born	175
Trusting in the Promise	54

U
Title	No.
Under the Cross	70

W
Title	No.
Waiting	67
We Answer the Call	52
What a Friend	97
What a Saviour	38
What Will You Do When the Saviour Comes?	136
What Will You Do With Jesus?	139
When I Survey	173
Where'er Thou Goest	184
Whiter than Snow	68
Who is on the Lord's Side?	55
Why Do You Wait?	129
Will You Come?	114
Wonderful Words of Life	157
Work, for the Night is Coming	86
Workers at Home	26

www.ingramcontent.com/pod-product-compliance
Lightning Source LLC
Chambersburg PA
CBHW030244170426
43202CB00009B/614